October, 2002

To Steve —

    "It is a majestic thing, thought Lincoln, for a person to be <u>responsible</u>." (see page 130)

    I've had this small volume for a few years — unread. The other night I found it, picked it up — and <u>read</u>!

    In the process, I was enriched — as deep in my innards (soul,) I felt ennobled.

    Still near the beginning of your own presidential endeavors, I wish for you the same kind of capture — and nobility.

            With my Love,
                Dad

ABRAHAM LINCOLN

Theologian of American Anguish

ABRAHAM LINCOLN

Theologian of American Anguish

Elton Trueblood

PROFESSOR-AT-LARGE EARLHAM COLLEGE

HARPER & ROW PUBLISHERS
New York, Evanston, San Francisco, London

Acknowledgment is made to the following publishers for permission to reprint from copyrighted material:

Harcourt Brace Jovanovich, Inc., *Abraham Lincoln, The War Years,* by Carl Sandburg.

Rutgers University Press, *The Collected Works of Abraham Lincoln,* edited by Roy P. Basler, 1953.

Sidgwick & Jackson Ltd., *Abraham Lincoln* by John Drinkwater.

STANDARD BOOK NUMBER: 06-063801-X

LIBRARY OF CONGRESS CATALOG CARD NUMBER: 72-79955

Designed by C. Linda Dingler

Contents

Preface

Hints dropped long ago by two Christian thinkers started me on the road to the eventual production of this book. One was my teacher, the other my friend, and now both are gone from us. The former was Willard L. Sperry, who was Dean of Harvard Divinity School in my time there, while the latter was Professor Reinhold Niebuhr, of Union Theological Seminary, New York. Both dealt, in conversation as well as in print, with Abraham Lincoln's theological acumen. Dean Sperry referred often to Lincoln as a theologian, saying, "He is one of the few men in history, our own history and all history, whose religion was great enough to bridge the gulfs between the sects, and to encompass us all." Reinhold Niebuhr rated the Civil War President as the most original of American religious thinkers. "Lincoln," he said, "has always been my hero in religion and in statecraft." Both of these scholars were convinced that professional theologians could learn much from a man who, while making no claim to theological competence, demonstrated genuine profundity concerning man and his relationship to God.

What I found difficult to resist, and what I did not really desire to resist, was the attraction of undoubted greatness. I noted Lord

Tweedsmuir's pithy remark, in justification of his producing a biography of Oliver Cromwell, when others already existed. "Every student of the seventeenth century in England, " he said, "must desire sooner or later to have his say about its greatest figure." The same holds true for everyone who cares about the American experiment. We know who the greatest figure is and we cannot leave him alone. If the contemporary student can add anything to the understanding of the deeper springs of Lincoln's character, no further justification is required.

One good reason for writing about Lincoln now is that there has been, in the recent past, an effort by some to denigrate his image and even to claim that the Emancipator was really a racist. This effort does not merit much attention, since the only truth in the attack is that which Lincoln scholars knew already, viz., that Lincoln was not simplistic either in his observations or in his conclusions. The critic, whether he be friendly or hostile, who approaches Abraham Lincoln with the assumption that he was a naïve idealist is bound to be disappointed.

Professor William J. Wolf of the Episcopal Theological Seminary in Cambridge, Massachusetts, has in his book, *Lincoln's Religion*, handled his subject so fairly that many difficult points of interpretation do not require further elaboration. "In the tangled forest of conflicting statements about Lincoln's religion or his lack of it," writes Wolf, "there are many pitfalls for the unwary." I am personally grateful to this scholar for pointing out some of the pitfalls which otherwise I might never have seen.

The present volume is devoted not primarily to Lincoln's religion, but to his religious *thinking*. No single writer can express Lincoln's greatness in its entirety, but when we deal seriously with his religious thinking we are getting close to the central mystery. The resource materials are so complex that the subject is at first bewildering to the student, but finally it is possible to achieve a measure of clarification.

The contemporary Lincoln student has the good fortune of being able to profit by the patient scholarship of Roy Basler and his colleagues, who made possible the publication, in 1953, of the definitive nine-volume *Collected Works of Abraham Lincoln*, published by Rutgers University Press, New Brunswick, New Jersey. I have had occasion to refer to this valuable resource so often that in footnotes I have abbreviated the title. In another fashion, every Lincoln student is indebted to John Nicolay and John Hay, Lincoln's devoted private secretaries, who brought out their ten volumes of *Abraham Lincoln: A History* in 1890. The name of this is abbreviated, also, being referred to in notes simply as Nicolay and Hay.

The books about Lincoln are so numerous that few can read them all, but, fortunately, this is not required. What is possible is the reading of what Lincoln himself wrote, and this is far more important. This is particularly true in regard to his religious ideas, where the firsthand witness is vastly preferable to the opinions of others, especially when they are speculative. In the man's written words, including both his letters and his speeches, we have the reliable evidence we need. No help in this regard has been greater than that provided by the Lincoln Library, associated with the Lincoln National Life Foundation, Fort Wayne, Indiana, and its librarian, Dr. R. Gerald McMurtry.

Like many Americans, I have honored Lincoln for a long time, but it is only in the last eight years that I have been able to immerse myself in his writings, wherever they could be found. The experience is one for which I am deeply and humbly grateful. The next best thing to being great is to walk with the great.

E. T.

Earlham College
Labor Day, 1972

ABRAHAM LINCOLN

Theologian of American Anguish

1
The Spiritual Pilgrimage of Abraham Lincoln

A great man lays upon posterity the duty of understanding him.

LORD TWEEDSMUIR

Only a few persons in human history have so towered above their contemporaries that they are universally recognized as belonging to the ages. One such person was born in a one-room cabin near Hodgenville, Kentucky, on February 12, 1809, and died, as the victim of an assassin's bullet, on April 15, 1865. The magnitude of this man's accomplishment has attracted so much attention that thousands of books and even entire libraries have been devoted to an effort to understand the mystery of his greatness. Though Lincoln is not easy to understand and though answers are never simple, he is more understandable today than ever before. The new possibility of understanding arises, in part, from the similarity between our time and his. Again there is in the American spirit deep division and consequent anguish. The chance that his thinking may illuminate our own is a good reason for its reexamination.

Lincoln's greatness was revealed in its fullness only at the end of the story, after months of turmoil not merely in the nation but in his own mind. While he is remembered primarily for his difficult political decisions which kept the Union intact, the more we study them the more we realize that all of them were reached at a level far deeper than that of politics. Underlying all particular decisions was a moral revulsion against human slavery, a mystical sense of the importance of the Union, and an abiding conviction that the divine order could be ascertained and followed. One of the most revealing items, as we search for the secret of Lincoln's achievement, is his letter to the Quaker woman Eliza Gurney, written September 4, 1864. In this message, addressed to a private person,[1] Lincoln expressed succinctly something of the anguish which he sensed in others and which reflected his own inner turmoil. "Your people," he wrote, "have had, and are having, a very great trial. On principle, and faith, opposed to both war and oppression, they can only practically oppose oppression by war." The difficulty was not that of following a moral principle at personal cost; the difficulty was that of knowing what to do when there is more than one principle, and when the principles clash.

It must be remembered that in the early autumn of 1864, when Lincoln wrote to Eliza Gurney, he was involved in a campaign for reelection, a campaign in which he was convinced, at that time, that he would be defeated. His political enemies were vicious in their criticism of his efforts to bring the war to an end, and it seriously appeared to many that the proponents of instant peace, without a solution of the problem, might win. So convinced of this was Lincoln that he wrote and sealed a letter to take effect on the occasion of the expected victory of his chief opponent, General George McClellan. The paper, which was secret

1. This letter is a prized possession of the Pennsylvania Historical Society in Philadelphia.

until the outcome of the election was known, was dated August 23, 1864, and read: "This morning, as for some days past, it seems exceedingly probable that this Administration will not be re-elected. Then it will be my duty to so cooperate with the President-elect, as to save the Union between the election and the inauguration; as he will have secured his election on such ground that he cannot possibly save it afterwards."

Increasingly, it is clear that the major key to Lincoln's greatness is his spiritual depth. His Second Inaugural, which has been widely acclaimed as the noblest state paper of the nineteenth century, is also recognized by those who study it carefully as a theological classic. The political sagacity rested in large measure upon a spiritual foundation.

To some people it seems strange to refer to Abraham Lincoln as a theologian. After all, his schooling was negligible; he was never a member of a church; certainly he did not think of himself as a professional in religious thinking. Far from being always confident, he passed through periods of uncertainty and doubt. In October, 1863, less than eighteen months before his death, he wrote: "I have often wished that I was a more devout man than I am." A major element in Lincoln's greatness was the way in which he could hold a strong moral position without the usual accompaniment of self-righteousness.

What is perhaps most strange of all is the magnitude of the difference which Lincoln was able to make in the religious life of the nation. It has been customary to speak of Lincoln as the "savior" of the Union, but we are nearer to the truth when we speak of him as its creator, since the Union became much more genuine as a result of his efforts than it had ever been before. Previous to Lincoln, the Union was still largely a dream, but he changed the entire picture by the character of his own commitment. There were many threats of secession before 1861, some coming even from New England, but after Lincoln such threats have not been seriously repeated. "The Civil War," said Dean Sperry, "has proved to be not so much the fortress where the Union was preserved as the fiery furnace where men were smelted together into one political stuff."[2]

The change in the national capital, after Lincoln, was striking. No longer was it a sleepy Southern town with occasional bursts of energy when Congress was in session. The nation henceforth possessed two striking new symbols, the dome on the hill and the memory of a man who cared supremely about the Union. What emerged was a new mystique, which has not been entirely lost in the subsequent years. Part of the mystique has arisen from the way in which Lincoln refused to be satisfied with simplistic answers. He had, in fact, as little sympathy with the instant abolitionists as he had with the apologists for slavery. Deeply convinced of the reality of the divine will, he had no patience at all with any who were perfectly sure that they knew the details of the divine will. His faith in the service which America, under God, might give to the world can be understood only when it is placed in the setting of the religious experience which came to dominate his nights and days.

The degree to which Lincoln set a new style in the national life is astonishing. Before his administration, there was a succession of Presidents who were reticent in expressing their hopes and fears in unapologetically religious terms. Some of these men were personally devout, but they hesitated to use the language of devotion when representing the nation. In contrast, Lincoln spoke openly, and with a striking absence of self-consciousness, of the dependence of the nation upon Providence. He was the first to establish a Federal Thanksgiving, which, though it had roots in colonial America, was not regularized until done so by him in the autumn of 1863. What is most surprising is that the

2. Willard L. Sperry, *The Meaning of God in the Life of Lincoln* (Boston: Central Church, 1922), p. 16.

novel pattern set by Lincoln has been followed by all of the men who have succeeded him in the highest office. The standard which he inaugurated, making it possible to refer to prayer and to divine guidance without embarrassment, has been continued to this day. The Federal Thanksgiving, according to which the life of devotion and the life of the nation are joined together, bears every evidence of being a permanent feature of our national existence. Professor Timothy L. Smith of Johns Hopkins University has pointed out that "the religious conviction which permeated Lincoln's statements and addresses set the tone for a new generation of public figures."[3]

The anguish which Lincoln experienced more than a century ago gave birth, not only to penitence and thanksgiving, but to much more that has endured in our spiritual panoply. The phrase "under God," which emerged spontaneously at the Gettysburg Battlefield in November, 1863, has now become an official part of our Salute to the Flag. "In God we trust," first used in Lincoln's administration, still adorns our coinage and is engraved on the walls of both houses of Congress. Out of anguish came greatness such as does not normally come in easier times.

The profundity of Lincoln's religious thinking which emerged during his days in the White House was not only new to the nation; it was also new to the man himself. One of the important features of Lincoln's theology is the fact that it was a *development*. The man had an amazing ability to grow! Lincoln, more than most persons, changed radically with the years and particularly with the heavy demands which events made upon him. He changed even in literary style. The most loyal reader of Lincoln's addresses is bound to admit that some of his early speaking and writing style was commonplace and pedestrian. There is very little in the early utterances to prepare us for the brilliance of the

3. *Revivalism and Social Reform* (Harper Torchbook, 1965), p. 39.

Message to Congress (December 1, 1862), the magnificent simplicity of the Gettysburg Address (November 19, 1863), and the profundity of the Second Inaugural (March 4, 1865). But before all of these masterpieces came the unforgettable "Meditation on the Divine Will," which has such a haunting quality that we can with difficulty put it down. As John Hay said, "It was not written to be seen of men," but it will be honored as long as men know what it is to suffer and to face difficult moral decisions.

The will of God prevails. In great contests each party claims to act in accordance with the will of God. Both *may* be, and one *must* be wrong. God can not be *for*, and *against*, the same thing at the same time. In the present civil war it is quite possible that God's purpose is something different from the purpose of either party—and yet the human instrumentalities, working just as they do, are of the best adaptation to effect His purpose. I am almost ready to say this is probably true—that God wills this contest, and wills that it shall not end yet. By His mere quiet power, on the minds of the now contestants, He could have either *saved* or *destroyed* the Union without a human contest. Yet the contest began. And having begun He could give the final victory to either side any day. Yet the contest proceeds.

The document is undated, but appears to have been written in September, 1862, after the deep disappointment of the Second Battle of Bull Run. It provides one of the best exhibitions of the theology of anguish. Attorney General Bates reported that early in September, 1862, Lincoln seemed "wrung by the bitterest anguish." The President, for some reason, left the meditation on his desk, where John Hay found it and copied it. As Sandburg has said, the sad man was "musing on the role of Providence in the dust of events."[4]

The spiritual level of the Meditation of 1862 is radically different from anything exhibited in the writings of the prairie years.

4. Carl Sandburg, *Abraham Lincoln, The War Years*, I (New York: Harcourt Brace Jovanovich, Inc., 1939), p. 590.

Indeed, it has been possible, by referring to early statements independent of later developments, to represent Lincoln as an unbeliever. But, by recognizing growth, we can save Lincoln from both his uncritical admirers and his uncritical detractors. There were a few hints of theological depth even in the years before the crucial autumn of 1862, but they are the exception rather than the rule. Lincoln's was the kind of mind which did not reach its true magnitude except in experiences of sorrow and of strain. Thus, in the emotional parting at the Springfield Railroad Station on February 11, 1861, Lincoln rose at least temporarily to a great height. "I now leave," he said, "not knowing when, or whether ever, I may return, with a task before me greater than that which rested upon Washington. Without the assistance of that Divine Being, who ever attended him, I cannot succeed. With that assistance I cannot fail. Trusting in Him, who can go with me, and remain with you and be everywhere for good, let us confidently hope that all will yet be well. To His care commending you, as I hope in your prayers you will commend me, I bid you an affectionate farewell."[5]

On the long journey to Washington, with numerous stops over a period of eleven days, the President-elect made many brief addresses, most of which are not really notable. An exception is provided in the unexpected phrase, depicting Americans as God's "almost chosen people," which was uttered at Trenton on February 21, 1861. Here the idea of a national vocation received one of its first clear expressions. The sentence which includes the surprise twist is: "I am exceedingly anxious that this Union, the Constitution, and the liberties of the people shall be perpetuated in accordance with the original idea for which that struggle was made, and I shall be most happy indeed if I shall be an humble instrument in the hands of the Almighty, and of this, his almost

5. The fact that the ending, as we now have it, is in Lincoln's own handwriting is evidence of the authenticity of this version.

chosen people, for perpetuating the object of that great struggle."

The struggle here mentioned was, in part, that of the American Revolution, but it was also something more. It was this extra which continued to haunt Lincoln as President until his last tragic days. The vision which was slowly becoming clarified was, he said, "something even more than National Independence; that something that held out a great promise to all the people of the world to all times to come." The vision, which transcended all mere nationalism, was becoming highly prophetic. Twenty months later, in the Annual Message to Congress of December 1, 1862, the dream was given an even sharper expression when the man born in a Kentucky cabin wrote, "We shall nobly save, or meanly lose, the last best hope of earth."

Very few expected the kind of greatness which emerged in Lincoln's final phase. Because we have known the climactic utterances all of our lives, many of us being able to repeat every word of the Gettysburg Address, it is difficult to understand the ridicule which Lincoln was forced to endure as he entered into the highest office. In an editorial the Baltimore *Sun* said, "Had we any respect for Mr. Lincoln, official or personal, as a man, or as President-elect of the United States, his career and speeches on his way to the seat of government would have cruelly impaired it." To make their harsh judgment even more clear the editors continued, "We do not believe the Presidency can ever be more degraded by any of his successors, than it has been by him, even before his inauguration."

What is especially obvious in Lincoln's spiritual pilgrimage is that the theological positions of his early manhood had little in common with those expressed at the end. Lincoln's career developed in five places, Kentucky, where he was born, southern Indiana, where he spent most of his boyhood, New Salem, Illinois, where he grew into full manhood, Springfield, Illinois, where he lived longest, and Washington, D.C., where he matured and died. Each of these places was important in his intellectual growth.

We know, chiefly because of the patient research of Dr. Louis A. Warren, of the group of Baptists with whom Thomas and Nancy Lincoln were associated before their removal to Indiana.[6] The most important fact is that they were strongly antislavery in conviction. In one of the best of several short autobiographies which Abraham Lincoln wrote,[7] he recognized the early influence of antislavery conviction as one reason for moving across the Ohio River. Referring to himself in the third person, Lincoln wrote:

> At this time his father resided on Knobcreek, on the road from Bardstown, Ky. to Nashville, Tenn. at a point three or three and a half miles South or South-West of Atherton's ferry on the Rolling Fork. From this place he removed to what is now Spencer county Indiana, in the autumn of 1816, A. then being in his eighth year. This removal was partly on account of slavery, but chiefly on account of the difficulty of land titles in Ky.

It is difficult to exaggerate the cultural poverty of Lincoln's formative years, from the age of seven to the age of twenty-one. By his own account, the Lincolns settled "in an unbroken forest," where, since the great task was "the clearing away of surplus wood," the boy "had an axe put into his hands at once." Lincoln recognized that "the family were originally Quakers," but since that connection was merely historical, Lincoln's father and stepmother both joined the Baptist congregation in their new neighborhood.

Pigeon Creek Baptist Church, affiliated with the denomination known as "Regular Baptists," was organized June 8, 1816, shortly before the Lincoln family arrived from Kentucky. The congregation met at first in their rude homes, but on Lincoln's eleventh birthday, February 12, 1820, plans for the meeting house were

6. *Lincoln's Youth, Seven to Twenty-one* (Indianapolis: Indiana Historical Society, 1959), pp. 13, 14.

7. This was written for John L. Scripps probably in June, 1860, to assist Scripps in the production of a campaign biography. See *Collected Works*, IV, pp. 60–67.

accepted. The building, which became very important to young Lincoln, was thirty feet long and twenty feet wide, of hewed logs. It was eight feet in the understory and six feet above the joists. They called it "Pigeon Meeting House." According to the records Thomas Lincoln joined by letter June 7, 1823, and "Sister Sally Lincoln by experience of grace," on April 8, 1826. When Nancy, Abraham's mother, died, in October, 1818, she was buried in the forest, but the grave of her daughter is in the yard adjacent to the meeting house. Because the teen-age Lincoln was appointed sexton, he had abundant opportunity to hear the itinerant preachers, who tended to be strongly antislavery.[8]

Lincoln's schooling was negligible, the aggregate, he said, not amounting to one year. In place of schooling, the boy had access to a few books which he read so faithfully that they left a permanent mark upon his mind, and helped to create the final elegance of his style. The chief books were the Bible, the plays of Shakespeare, Daniel Defoe's *Robinson Crusoe*, John Bunyan's *Pilgrim's Progress*, Aesop's *Fables*, the *Autobiography of Benjamin Franklin*, and Weems' *Life of Washington*, the influence of these books upon his later thought and style of expression being evident at many points. When, for example, Lincoln spoke at Trenton, New Jersey, on February 21, 1861, he referred to his boyhood reading of the *Life of Washington* and revealed how that experience had aroused in his young mind a sense of the nobility of the total movement of which he was a part. "I recollect thinking then," he said, "boy even though I was, that there must have been something more than common that those men struggled for."

We know part of the secret of Lincoln's greatness when we notice that the books which formed his early taste for literature were, on the whole, far removed from the trivial. Thereby, the lack of formal education was partly balanced by what Professor

8. For details see *Lincoln Lore*, No. 661.

Whitehead has called "the habitual vision of greatness." Weems may not have been a wholly reliable author, but the greatness of the man whom he depicted shone through and reached the boy in his rude forest home. Lincoln said of his education, in his autobiographical fragment of 1860, "What he has in the way of education, he has picked up." After he had settled in New Salem and was twenty-three years of age, he was encouraged by Mentor Graham[9] to undertake a study of English grammar, a task which gave him something which a college education might not have provided. If he had attended Illinois College, as once seemed possible, it is hard to believe that the outcome would have been on the level of the style of thought and speech which actually emerged. Certainly it would not have been the same. He said he regretted his want of education and "does what he can to supply the want."

In his effort to reach a rational theology, Lincoln as a young man had very little real help. There was no church at New Salem, and few of his neighbors cared greatly about ideas. Though the deep sense of reverence which had developed in the Indiana forest seems never to have left the young man, he began to speculate in ways which made some people think of him as verging on infidelity. Certainly he was influenced for a time by the amateur philosophizing of his pioneer neighbors, as he revolted against the ignorant preaching which he heard from time to time. As a young boy in Indiana, he had enjoyed mimicking the hell-fire and brimstone preachers of the raw frontier. "On Monday mornings he would mount a stump, and deliver, with a wonderful approach to exactness the sermon he had heard the day before."[10]

9. Local schoolmaster and leading Baptist at New Salem, Graham shared Lincoln's intellectual interests. Lincoln lived at Graham's house in 1833 and was reputedly helped by the older man in his public speaking.

10. Ward Hill Lamon, *The Life of Abraham Lincoln*, p. 39.

In Illinois Lincoln was repulsed by the crude emotionalism of the annual revivals, including those conducted by his political rival, Peter Cartwright. Lincoln, being naturally alienated by the fierce competition between denominational groups, experienced some sympathy with those who, by their opponents, were termed "infidels." His law partner in Springfield, William H. Herndon, emphasized this connection grotesquely, even going so far as to say, "Now let it be written in history and on Mr. Lincoln's tomb: 'He died an unbeliever.'" No serious modern historian accepts this as true. If it is true, we are forced to the conclusion that Lincoln was the arch-hypocrite. His hundreds of statements affirming the reality of God's guidance would have to be assigned to insincerity, a task too great even for the most inveterate debunker.

The slender thread of truth on which Herndon wove his thesis is not really very surprising. What it amounts to is that, in his New Salem days, the young Lincoln apparently read the *Age of Reason* by Thomas Paine and Volney's *Ruins*. These were, of course, discussed around the fire in the evenings. In the winter of 1831–1832, a debating society was formed with Lincoln as a participating member. The young man's brilliant mind made him delight in taking any side in a debate, but it is highly unreasonable to conclude that positions taken in this fashion reflected his own enduring convictions.

Herndon claimed that Lincoln, in his New Salem period, wrote a book defending infidelity, the book being lost.[11] There has never been any conclusive evidence about this supposed book, but whatever plausibility the story once had was undermined by the discovery, after ninety-six years, of Lincoln's own statement in which he denied that he had ever held an "infidel"

11. A careful consideration of the "lost book" is provided by William J. Wolf, *Lincoln's Religion* (Philadelphia: Pilgrim Press, 1970), pp. 45–47.

position. The statement, which brought one long controversy to an end, is a handbill printed on July 31, 1846. It was found by Dr. Henry E. Pratt, executive secretary of the Abraham Lincoln Association, and was published in the March, 1942, number of the *Abraham Lincoln Quarterly*. Dr. Pratt's discovery represented one of the major advances of the century in Lincoln scholarship. The handbill is so important for the understanding of Lincoln that it calls for reproduction in its entirety:

To The Voters of the Seventh Congressional District Fellow Citizens:

A charge having got into circulation in some of the neighborhoods of this District, in substance that I am an open scoffer at Christianity, I have by the advice of some friends concluded to notice the subject in this form. That I am not a member of any Christian Church, is true; but I have never denied the truth of the Scripture; and I have never spoken with intentional disrespect of religion in general, or of any denomination of Christians in particular. It is true that in early life I was inclined to believe in what I understand is called the "Doctrine of Necessity"— that is, that the human mind is impelled to action, or held in rest by some power, over which the mind itself has no control; and I have sometimes (with one, two or three, but never publicly) tried to maintain this opinion in argument—The habit of arguing thus however, I have, entirely left off for more than five years—And I add here, I have always understood this same opinion to be held by several of the Christian denominations. The foregoing, is the whole truth, briefly stated, in relation to myself upon this subject.

I do not think I could myself, be brought to support a man for office, whom I knew to be an open enemy of, and scoffer at, religion. Leaving the higher matter of eternal consequences, between him and his Maker, I still do not think any man has the right thus to insult the feelings, and injure the morals, of a community in which he may live. If, then I was guilty of such conduct, I should blame no man who should condemn me for it; but I do blame those, whoever they may be, who falsely put such a charge in circulation against me.

The handbill clarifies many points. For one thing it shows that what Lincoln called the "Doctrine of Necessity" was an important feature of his developing world view. Apparently, what he referred to was the idea of determinism, according to which all events are explained as necessary consequences of prior causes. The basic flaw in this philosophy, and the chief reason why Lincoln, with his clear mind, could not long uphold it, is that it makes impossible any genuine responsibility. Men are certainly not responsible for that which they cannot avoid doing, just as the stone is not responsible for the death of a person who is killed by its movement. There is abundant evidence that Lincoln valued supremely the sense of personal responsibility and the freedom of decision without which it is meaningless. Accordingly, the agony of decision came to be more and more important in his life. On the other hand, however, he never left off one element in the idea of necessity, viz., that our destinies are not wholly of our own making.

The determinism about which the young men of New Salem sometimes debated was not far removed from the doctrine of predestination which Lincoln had heard expounded so often in his Pigeon Creek boyhood. Slowly and painfully this conception was purged of its crudities, until what remained was the mature conviction expressed in the Second Inaugural. In this, we observe, Lincoln did not refer to "necessity" or to "determinism," but he did affirm his abiding conviction that the destinies of men and nations are not wholly within their own hands. After the fiery trial and the anguish of experience, something which differed from both determinism and voluntarism was envisioned and accepted. It was this position, so much richer than compromise, which fascinated the late eminent theologian Reinhold Niebuhr. "This combination," he said, "of moral resoluteness about the immediate issues with a religious awareness of another dimension of meaning and judgment must be regarded as almost a perfect model of the difficult but not impossible task of remaining loyal and responsible toward the moral treasures of a free civilization on the one hand while yet having some religious vantage point over the struggle."[12]

A second clarification which the handbill provides is the precise dating of the change which came in Lincoln's own thinking. According to the handbill, a major change occurred in 1841, when Lincoln was thirty-two years of age. We can now see that the fundamental chapters in Abraham Lincoln's life, after his childhood, were four. The first chapter takes him to the age of thirty-two; the second, a period of twenty years, ends with his departure for Washington, in February, 1861; the third ends with the autumn of 1862, when he had been in the White House during a year and a half of unrelieved frustration; the fourth and last, occupying two and half years, carries him to the assassination.

The change in 1841 was a radical one. He had already been settled in Springfield for four years, had practiced law, and had served in the Illinois legislature, but this measure of success had not been sufficient to give him any real peace of mind. In a period of self-doubt and dire despair Lincoln broke his first engagement with Mary Todd. His decision, at the beginning of 1841, was influenced both by the fear that Miss Todd might not be happy in sharing his humble station and the further fear that her aristocratic relatives "looked with much disfavor on the match."[13] The young man's act was not disgraceful, but the entire experience was one of anguish.

In a letter addressed to his law partner, John T. Stuart, on January 20, 1841, Lincoln wrote: "I have, within the last few days, been making a most discreditable exhibition of myself in

12. *The Irony of American History* (New York: Charles Scribner's Sons, 1952), p. 172.
13. See *Lincoln Lore*, No. 707.

the way of hypochondriaism."[14] Three days later he wrote: "I am now the most miserable man living. If what I feel were equally distributed to the whole human family, there would not be one cheerful face on the earth. Whether I shall ever be better I cannot tell; I awfully forebode I shall not. To remain as I am is impossible."[15] As late as March 27, 1842, in writing to his friend Joshua Speed, he referred to "that fatal first of Jany. '41." He might have been happy, in subsequent months, he said, "but for the never-absent idea, that there is *one* still unhappy whom I have contributed to make so."[16]

The key to Lincoln's famous employment of humor is not that he failed to appreciate the tragic aspects of human existence, but rather that he felt these with such keenness that some relief was required. "If I couldn't tell these stories I would die," he told a worried Ohio congressman who had come to protest General George McClellan's handling of the Army of the Potomac. Isaac N. Arnold was one of his close associates who saw clearly, in Lincoln, the combination of characteristics of an opposite nature. "Mirthfulness and melancholy, hilarity and sadness, were," he said, "strangely combined in him. His mirth was sometimes exuberant. It sparked in jest, story and anecdote, while at the next moment, his peculiarly sad, pathetic melancholy eyes would seem to wander far away, and one realized that he was a man 'familiar with sorrow and acquainted with grief.' " Andrew D. White, later the famous President of Cornell University, said "his face seemed to me one of the saddest I have ever seen."

Part of the paradox lies in the fact that the teller of humorous tales vastly preferred tragic poetry to any other. Reading Shakespeare's plays in the Indiana cabin, he came to love *Macbeth*, *Hamlet*, *Richard III*, and *King John*, so that he could repeat effort-

14. *Collected Works*, I, p. 228.
15. Ibid., p. 229.
16. Ibid., p. 282.

lessly long passages, even during the strain of the war years. On April 9, 1865, steaming up the Potomac, only five days before his assassination, Lincoln deliberately guided the conversation to literary subjects and read aloud from Shakespeare for several hours to his companions.

After 1841 Lincoln was equidistant from the heresy which makes a person believe that he can do nothing, and the opposite heresy which makes him suppose that he is the master of his own fate. He was working out a philosophy which was deep enough to include both foreordination and free will. The third way, which differed from both fatalism and voluntarism, was, in essence, a theory of divine vocation. More and more this became the foundation upon which Lincoln built the superstructure of his thought. The idea of vocation, of course, involves paradox, but there is no possibility of understanding Lincoln's mind if paradox is eliminated.

Because to his friend Speed Lincoln could write with utter honesty and with no necessity to impress the electorate, the letter of July 4, 1842, is of major significance. In the course of this letter he wrote, "I believe God made me one of the instruments of bringing your Fanny and you together, which union, I have no doubt He had fore-ordained."[17] As early as July, 1842, Lincoln had recovered his confidence in himself by reaching a conviction of God's guidance. "Stand *still* and see the salvation of the Lord" was, he said, his text for the moment. Out of his continuous reading of the Old Testament, the tortured man was able to draw, for personal application, the words of Moses to the people (Exodus 14:13). By this time he and Mary Todd were engaged again, and they were married exactly four months later, November 4, 1842.

An important element in the new beginning of 1841 was a gift

17. Ibid., p. 289.

to Lincoln from Speed's mother-in-law of a new Bible. In a letter to Mary Speed, written September 27, 1841, Lincoln said, "Tell your mother that I have not got her 'present' with me; but that I intend to read it regularly when I return home. I doubt not that it is really, as she says, the best cure for the 'Blues' could one but take it according to the truth."[18] Many years later, in the White House, Lincoln autographed his photograph with the words: "For Mrs. Lucy G. Speed, from whose pious hand I accepted the present of an Oxford Bible twenty years ago." Whatever the cause of his cure, the important fact is that it occurred. Accordingly, in a letter to Joshua Speed, written at Springfield February 3, 1842, Lincoln said, "I have been quite clear of hypo since you left,—even better than I was along in the fall."[19] Life did not become easy, but after 1841 it was different.

The relatively tranquil period of Lincoln's life covering the twenty years up to his departure from Springfield as President-elect was sharply pierced by the death of Eddie, the second son of Abraham and Mary Lincoln. The death of this little boy, not yet four years old, on February 1, 1850, produced a second spiritual crisis comparable in its results to that which came nine years earlier. On February 23, 1850, Lincoln wrote to his step-brother, John D. Johnston, "I suppose you had not learned that we lost our little boy. He was sick fifty two days & died the morning of the first day of this month."[20]

Consequent to the new crisis was the friendship of Dr. James Smith, pastor of the First Presbyterian Church of Springfield. Dr. Smith was a well-educated Scotsman, the author of a book, *The Christian's Defense*. Lincoln had never before encountered a proponent of the Christian faith of Smith's intellectual strength and distinction. When the Lincolns were forlorn in the loss of

18. Ibid., p. 261.
19. Ibid., p. 268.
20. *Collected Works*, II, pp. 76, 77.

their child, Dr. Smith reached them at their point of greatest need. At Eddie's funeral the pastor preached the sermon and soon, thereafter, at his suggestion, Mary Lincoln joined the First Presbyterian Church. Mr. Lincoln did not join with his wife, but attended Divine Worship with the degree of regularity which his roving life permitted. Already it was obvious that both those who afterward called him an atheist and those who claimed that he was an orthodox Christian were demonstrably wrong. He believed, but he did not believe lightly or conventionally. The death of his son sufficed to eliminate forever the lighthearted irreverence of his youth.

Something of the new faith which came following the death of Eddie is indicated by the message which he wrote to his stepbrother, when his father was dying:

I sincerely hope father may recover his health, but at all events, tell him to remember to call upon and confide in our great and good merciful Maker, who will not turn away from him in any extremity. He notes the fall of a sparrow and numbers the hairs of our heads, and He will not forget the dying man who puts his trust in Him.

A new emphasis, different from anything expressed in Lincoln's earlier statements, was that concerning life after death. The letter continued:

Say to him that if we could meet now it is doubtful whether it would not be more painful than pleasant, but that if it be his lot to go now, he will soon have a joyous meeting with many loved ones gone before, and where the rest of us, through the help of God, hope ere long to join them.[21]

In this middle period of his life Lincoln did not claim that all of his doubts were swept away, for they had not been. One of the most appealing of his utterances, confided to a neighbor, bore

21. Ibid., pp. 96, 97.

exactly on this point. "Probably it is to be my lot to go on in a twilight, feeling and reasoning my way through life, as questioning, doubting Thomas did. But in my poor maimed, withered way, I bear with me as I go on a seeking spirit of desire for a faith that was with him of olden time, who, in his need, as I in mine, exclaimed, 'Help thou my unbelief.' "[22]

The anguish and turmoil of Lincoln's mind never ended. When, toward the end of the Springfield period, people began to mention Lincoln as a possible occupant of the highest office, the man himself was doubtful, considering himself inadequate for the magnitude of the responsibility. Thus, in a letter written July 28, 1859, he said, "I must say I do not think myself fit for the Presidency." What roused him out of a certain lethargy was the slavery issue. In a brief autobiography, written December 20, 1859, he said, "I was losing interest in politics, when the repeal of the Missouri Compromise aroused me again." In his adamant stand against the extension of slavery into hitherto free territories, he began to feel that he was indeed an instrument of the divine will. Never claiming certainty, he lived by hope and entered the conflict with a confidence which sustained him. "I do hope," he said at Clinton, Illinois, on October 14, 1859, "that as there is a just and righteous God in Heaven, our principles will and shall prevail sooner or later."

Increasingly, whether in religion or in politics, Lincoln occupied an embattled middle ground. As in religion he had to fight on two fronts, so he fought in the political arena. His position was naturally criticized as much by the militant Abolitionists as it was by the militant proponents of the extension of slavery. Even to this day there are writers, including theological ones,

22. Henry B. Rankin, *Personal Recollections of Abraham Lincoln* (New York: G. P. Putnam's Sons, 1916), pp. 324, 325. Though not all of Rankin's recollections are consistent with other known evidence, this testimony of Rankin's mother appears to be reliable and has been much admired.

who claim to be shocked when they discover that Lincoln did not affirm the factual equality of the races. He did not claim this because it was not the point at issue. The question, he said over and over, is not what a man's particular abilities may be, but what his rights are as a human being made in God's image. He listened to the arguments of the proslavery party, especially the argument that slavery was good for the slave. The peculiarity of slavery, he said, consists of the fact "that it is the only good thing which no man ever seeks the good of, *for himself.*"[23]

More and more Lincoln dealt with the problem of human slavery, not merely on the political level, but upon a far deeper one. Thus, at New Haven, Connecticut, on March 6, 1860, he said, "We think Slavery a great moral wrong, and while we do not claim the right to touch it where it exists, we wish to treat it as a wrong in the Territories, where our votes will reach it. We think that a respect for ourselves, a regard for future generations and for the God that made us, require that we put down this wrong where our votes will properly reach it."[24] This position did not satisfy the Abolitionists any more than it satisfied the slave party, but Lincoln followed it because he was keenly aware of the limitations which fidelity to the Constitution imposed. As an instrument of the divine will he was devoted to the possible! This decision required that emphasis be placed upon *extension.* This is why, after he was elected, Lincoln wrote to Alexander H. Stephens as follows: "You think slavery is *right* and ought to be extended; while we think it is *wrong* and ought to be restricted. That I suppose is the rub. It certainly is the only substantial difference between us."[25] Two and a half months later, these same words were employed in Lincoln's First Inaugural Ad-

23. This is part of a fragment to which Nicolay and Hay gave the date October 1, 1858.
24. *Collected Works,* IV, p. 16.
25. Ibid., p. 160.

dress, delivered March 4, 1861. Much as he was convinced that slavery was wrong, he rejected the argument that it should therefore be attacked by force where it was legally established. Emancipation was right on principle, but peaceful union was also right on principle. Hating both oppression and war, in the words of his letter to Mrs. Gurney, he sought a way in which oppression could finally be ended without war. "In your hands, my dissatisfied fellow countrymen, and not in *mine*, is the momentous issue of civil war. The government will not assail *you*. You can have no conflict, without being yourselves the aggressors. *You* have no oath registered in Heaven to destroy the government, while I shall have the most solemn one to 'preserve, protect, and defend' it."

From the day when these words were uttered, the augustness of the oath became more and more important in Lincoln's thinking. It seemed to him that the taking of the oath lifted the struggle out of the level of politics into the level of the holy. At no point did this become more clear than in the Cabinet meeting held on September 22, 1862. Lincoln, who had actually written an Emancipation Proclamation two months earlier, explained his decision to emancipate slaves in all territories then in rebellion against the federal government. In sharp contrast to the mood with which the meeting had begun, the President, feeling that he was treading upon holy ground, became extremely solemn. "I made," he said, "a solemn vow before God, that if General Lee was driven back from Pennsylvania, I would crown the result by the declaration of freedom to the slaves." We are chiefly indebted, for our knowledge of these words, to Francis B. Carpenter, the artist who lived in the White House while he worked on the well-known painting which depicts the reading of the Proclamation to the Cabinet. Carpenter's report is corroborated by that of Secretary Salmon P. Chase, who described the eventful meeting in his diary. The key words of Lincoln are: "When the Rebel

Army was at Frederick, I determined, as soon as it should be driven out of Maryland, to issue a Proclamation of Emancipation, such as I thought most likely to be useful. I said nothing to anyone, but I made a promise to myself and (hesitating a little) to my Maker. The Rebel Army is now driven out, and I am going to fulfill that promise." Another confirmation comes from the diary of Gideon Welles, the Secretary of the Navy. Referring to Lincoln, Welles wrote, "He had, he said, made a vow, a covenant, that if God gave us the victory in the approaching battle (which had just been fought) he would consider it his duty to move forward in the cause of emancipation." God, Lincoln said, "had decided this question in favor of the slave." After that day in the autumnal equinox of 1862, there was much more anguish for Americans, both in the North and in the South, but the course was set. The spiritual pilgrimage of Abraham Lincoln had reached the beginning of the end.

2
The Agonizing Interlude

*It is a momentous thing to be the instrument, under Providence,
of the liberation of a race.*

ABRAHAM LINCOLN

There are many mysteries about the life of Abraham Lincoln,
but no mystery is greater than that of the radical change which
occurred in his public work after he had entered the White
House. The change, which is evident in many ways, is most
obvious in the realm of public discourse. The style of his last
great utterances, beginning with the "Meditation on the Divine
Will" in September, 1862, is of a totally different character from
anything which Lincoln produced in previous years. The First
Inaugural had a certain grandeur, but the sentences most often
quoted, at the end, were partly the work of Seward. It was only
after he took office, and after the terrible sense of division in his
beloved country had fully come upon him, that totally new and
unsuspected powers began to be made manifest.

Did Lincoln recognize a change in himself? Apparently so. He
told Noah Brooks, the man who would have become his personal
secretary had he lived, that "his own election to office, and the

crisis immediately following, influentially determined him in what he called 'a process of crystallization' going on in his mind." It is not that we can assign an exact date for the change, since the President could not do so himself, but we can at least say that a new spirit was dominant after the middle of 1862. One evidence of the new firmness of conviction is that when Lincoln first shared with his Cabinet the plan of emancipation, on July 22, 1862, instead of asking their advice, he *informed* them. By that time the sad, contemplative man had been at the center of the storm for nearly a year and a half, and in that period he had changed from an Illinois politician into a world statesman.

The new Lincoln, though alive to many issues, was devoted primarily to the achievement of freedom for all. As we cannot rightly understand his opposition to slavery if we think of it as a merely political position, neither can we understand it if it is stated in only moral terms. His entire conception of morality was *derivative*, because he did not believe in an independent order of moral values. "The good for Lincoln," as Professor Wolf has so clearly said, "was ultimately anchored in the will of God, not subject to human likes or dislikes."[1]

Most of 1861 was for Lincoln, as for the nation, a very bad time. Even after the die was cast by the attack on Fort Sumter and the very life of the nation endangered, the new chief executive had to spend much of his time dealing with office-seekers. Wherever he turned he found men who were thinking not of the national crisis, and not of the liberation of the slaves, but of their own personal careers in office. When the military struggle actually began, the news was almost wholly bad so far as the prospects of the Union forces were concerned. On the night following the Battle of Bull Run in July, 1861, Lincoln "lay awake," said his secretaries, "on a sofa in the Executive office."[2]

Already in the midst of the discouragement and the apparent

1. William J. Wolf, *Lincoln's Religion*, p. 91.
2. Nicolay and Hay, IV, p. 368.

indecision of his first year in the highest office, Lincoln was placing the struggle in a larger context and mentioning "the whole family of man." "The issue," he said, "embraces more than the fate of these United States. It presents to the whole family of man the question of whether a constitutional republic, or democracy—a government of the people by the same people—can or can not maintain its territorial integrity against its own domestic foes."[3] The seed of the Gettysburg Address was planted.

During his first year as President, Lincoln was faced with public criticism of a bitterness which is hard to believe. All men in public life are forced to bear abuse, but few have faced as much as Lincoln faced day after day. The writers in the newspapers could sound smart because they did not have the responsibilities of decision, and they could sound bold by enunciating extreme positions which they were not required to implement. Lincoln, by contrast, in order to maintain integrity had to reject extremes because he was sworn to be faithful to the welfare of the entire nation.

As the months of anguish and apparent failure wore on, the cruel criticism of Lincoln in the Northern states came from opposite directions. On the one hand, there developed the party of radicals, whom John Hay cleverly labeled "Jacobins." They constantly criticized Lincoln for not pushing the war more vigorously, crying "On to Richmond." Hay applied the term used in the French Revolution because of the similarity of mood, if not of doctrine. A major mouthpiece of this kind of criticism was the New York *Independent*.[4]

From the opposite side came the criticism expressed by the "peace" party, popularly labeled "Copperheads." This term

3. Message to Congress in Special Session, July 4, 1861. *Collected Works*, IV, p. 426.
4. See T. Harry Williams, *Lincoln and the Radicals* (Madison: University of Wisconsin Press, 1960).

came into general use in the crucial autumn of 1862 and was applied to those who, believing it was impossible for the Union forces to conquer the Confederacy, sought a political compromise and opposed the war measures which Lincoln felt he had to uphold if the Union was to be preserved. It is hard to know which of the two major kinds of criticism wounded the sensitive Lincoln the more. Lincoln listened to his critics, but as he fought the battle of his own mind, he became convinced that he dared not capitulate to either the Copperhead or the Jacobin. The price in terms of his own peace of mind, however, was high.

The early weeks of 1862 were dark indeed, partly because of the death of Willie, who was undoubtedly the President's favorite child. Willie died in the White House on February 20, 1862, at the age of eleven. In some ways the sorrow was like that produced by the death of Eddie twelve years earlier, but the new sadness was enhanced by the constant sense of the national tragedy which had not been present when the first death occurred in 1850. Lincoln's melancholy after Willie died was so deep that it seemed impossible to believe that the old buoyancy would ever return. The depression seemed complete! Yet, by midsummer, there was a new spirit in the man, marked by a confidence from which he never again retreated.

Of all of the interpreters of Lincoln no one has expressed the change better than did the late Nathaniel W. Stephenson. "Out of this strange period of intolerable confusion," he wrote, "a gigantic figure had at last emerged. The outer and the inner Lincoln had fused. He was now a coherent personality, masterful in spite of his gentleness, with his own peculiar fashion of self-reliance, having a policy of his own devising, his colors nailed upon the masthead."[5] We cannot, of course, know precisely what went on in Abraham Lincoln's soul in the dreadful winter of 1862, but we do know something of what emerged.

5. *Lincoln* (Indianapolis: The Bobbs-Merrill Company, 1922), p. 257.

When President Lincoln was at the lowest point of his grief, in the late winter of 1862, one visitor to the White House made a lasting difference. This was Dr. Francis Vinton, rector of Trinity Church, New York.[6] The insight which Dr. Smith had given the Lincolns in Springfield twelve years before was reaffirmed and made more intelligible by the spiritual help which Dr. Vinton offered the bereaved couple. His help came by the intellectual route, the only way in which it could come to Abraham Lincoln. The visitor showed that it is wholly rational for God to continue His interest in and concern for persons after the death of the body, just as before. Dr. Vinton called attention to Christ's own teaching on this point, especially as it is reported in Luke 20:38, "For he is not a God of the dead, but of the living: for all live unto him."

This approach seemed utterly fresh, as the rector of Trinity expounded it. Lincoln was struck especially by the visitor's confident words, "Your son is *alive*."[7] As the President pondered, his entire outlook began to change for he realized that God cannot be defeated. If God cannot be defeated by the death of a little boy, it is also true that He cannot be defeated by a civil war. Ida Tarbell's insight at this point is as follows: "It was the first experience of his life, so far as we know, which drove him to look outside of his own mind and heart for help to endure a personal grief. It was the first time in his life when he had not been sufficient for his own experience."[8] If there had not been the darkness of the late winter of 1862, it is not likely that there would have been the amazing burst of light at the end of the year. As he had done before, Lincoln matured best in sorrow. Miss Tarbell neglects the earlier experiences, especially those of 1841,

6. Our most reliable account of this visit is provided by the artist Francis B. Carpenter in his book, *Six Months in the White House.*

7. Learning that Dr. Vinton had published a sermon on eternal life, Lincoln asked that a copy be sent to him. Carpenter said he read it many times.

8. *The Life of Abraham Lincoln*, II, p. 92.

but her emphasis upon Lincoln's recognition of his own inadequacy is helpful. The profound paradox is that the great man became more confident in his approach to other men, including the men of his own Cabinet, when he recognized that his major confidence was not in himself but in Another.

That the new and stronger mood was the result of a fundamentally mystical experience is the conviction of one of the most thorough of Lincoln scholars, the late Nathaniel Stephenson. "Lincoln's final emergence," he says, "was a deeper thing than merely the consolidation of a character, the transformation of a dreamer into a man of action. The fusion of the outer and the inner person was the result of a profound interior change. Those elements of mysticism which were in him from the first, which had gleamed daily through such deep over-shadowing, were at last established in their permanent form."[9]

Central to the new spiritual development was an enlargement of the idea of vocation. Less and less did the President think that he was acting merely in his own will or depending upon his own meager resources. "Hate, fear, jealousy," as Sandburg put it, "were rampant"[10] in the summer, but that was not by any means the total story, for Lincoln grew immeasurably as he came to think of himself as an "instrument" of God's will. He needed an idea of this magnitude to keep him going in the face of unjust criticism as well as of military defeat. The sense that there really is a Guiding Hand, which makes possible a genuine calling for both individuals and nations, gave a tremendous new sense of moral strength. It was not enough to watch events and to muddle along day by day. What was much more important, Lincoln came to believe, was the effort to discern a pattern beneath the seeming

9. Stephenson, *Lincoln*, p. 261. The reader who wishes to see a brief statement of Stephenson's conclusions is advised to study his essay on Lincoln in the *Encyclopaedia Britannica*, 14th edition, Vol. 14.

10. Sandburg, *Abraham Lincoln, The War Years*, I, p. 501.

irrationality of events. He had come really to believe that God molds history and that He employs erring mortals to effect His purpose.

The final position of political mysticism which Lincoln reached as a solution of his intellectual problem was equally removed from two extreme positions. On the one hand, it was far removed from the arrogant nationalism which assumes that God is on our side. Lincoln's concern, he said, was whether he was on God's side. He did not identify the will of his own fallible administration with the will of Almighty God, because he saw everything, including his own Presidency, proceeding under judgment. On the other hand, Lincoln did not admire those who think it is a mark of sophistication to sneer at patriotism. He believed that God has a will for a country and that an honest man should rejoice in the effort to try to remake his country after the divine pattern, insofar as this pattern is revealed to him. He loved his country devoutly; he believed it had been brought into existence for a purpose; he believed that this purpose had something to do with the ultimate welfare of mankind.

There is no doubt that the early months of 1862 were months of indecision for President Lincoln. The clamor of voices urged him in many contradictory directions. He was told that any move to free the slaves would be disastrous, particularly in the border states; he was told that failure to free the slaves would cause him to lose European support. He was tormented in a manner hard to bear by senators who considered themselves wiser than the President and who, accordingly, organized the Committee on the Conduct of the War. The problems of finding able generals seemed insoluble. McClellan's retreat to the James River after the Seven Days' Battles near Richmond was an event which shook Union confidence.

Then, quite suddenly, in July, 1862, a new quality of presidential leadership became evident and continued to the tragic end.

The ebb tide of Lincoln's moral energy had ended. One vivid evidence of the new firmness is that before the year was over Lincoln, on November 5, relieved General McClellan of his command. The best way for us to know what was transpiring is for us to listen, not primarily to others, but to Lincoln himself. "It had got to be mid-summer of 1862," he told Carpenter. "Things had gone . . . from bad to worse, until I felt that we had reached the end of our rope on the plan . . . we had been pursuing; that we must change our tactics or lose the game."

As we study now the events of these crucial months, we can see something of how the light arose. "History," says Bruce Catton, "does not usually make real sense until long afterward." For example, we know the effectiveness of an official message, written by English Quakers and transmitted to the President through Francis T. King of Baltimore. Lincoln wrote to King and his associates on January 7, 1862, acknowledging the receipt of "the Memorial of the English Friends." One reason for Lincoln's respect for the judgment of English Friends was his admiration for John Bright, the most eminent of them at that period. "Although I trust," he wrote, "that any fears entertained of serious derangement of our amicable relations have been without foundation, I cannot but gratefully appreciate your prompt and generous suggestions in the interests of peace and humanity."[11]

The Memorial, addressed to the British Government, was written December 9 and was signed by forty-one members of the Meeting for Sufferings.[12] By printing and distributing the document, the English Quakers hoped to influence their Government to seek a peaceful solution of the issues then separating America and Great Britain. The nub of the controversy was the Union blockade of Confederate ports, which severely affected England's supply of cotton. In his handling of the "Trent" affair, Lincoln

11. *Collected Works,* V, p. 92.
12. The three-page printed document is in Friends House Library, London.

had gone out of his way to soothe British irritation, but there was still more Southern sentiment in England than in any other European country. In the wave of anti-Union feeling, John Bright was almost the only major statesman who supported Lincoln's firm policy.[13] Lord Palmerston wanted to see America divided, with consequent weakness, and even Gladstone said publicly that the success of the Confederacy was already assured. It was as a counterpoise to such sentiment that the Quaker memorial said:

There are, perhaps, no two independent nations on the face of the earth so closely united together as England and America by the combined ties of blood, of language, of religion, of constitutional freedom, and of commercial interest; and no two nations between whom a war would be a more open scandal to our common Christianity, or a more serious injury to the welfare and progress of the human race.

Such words were exactly suited to Lincoln's mentality and to his moral stance. Coming as they did early in his year of decision, they helped to stiffen his determination and to heighten his confidence. He understood thoroughly the real danger that the British Government might support the Confederacy and that, if this should occur, France would follow suit. In this delicate situation the knowledge that John Bright and his fellow Quakers were sympathetic with Lincoln's purposes gave him moral undergirding. On a portrait of Lincoln Bright wrote, "And if there be on earth and among men any 'Divine' right to govern, surely it rests with the Ruler so chosen and so appointed." Much as Lincoln sensed God's guidance, he valued also the support of such a man.

Before entering the White House Lincoln had understood the evil character of human slavery, but in the agonizing months which followed his inauguration he came to see a still bigger

13. Bright had, however, the strong support of Queen Victoria and the Prince Consort. Prince Albert's effort to secure an alteration in the peremptory dispatch to Lincoln was the last act of his life. He died December 14, 1861.

issue, of which the slavery issue was only one part. This was the issue of the perpetuation of the ideal of democracy. As 1862 wore on, the sharpening of the intellectual position became more evident until it reached a climax in the Message to Congress on December 1. What Lincoln was producing, in the months when some thought that he was doing very little, was an intellectual and spiritual clarification of the importance, for the whole world, of the American experiment in government.

When in July, 1862, Lincoln's new pattern of confidence suddenly appeared, he had just had another Quaker connection which bore upon his momentous decision. Three men and three women, official representatives of what were called "Progressive Friends," waited on the President on June 20, 1862. The chief purpose of their visit was that of urging immediate emancipation. In the dialogue which followed the presentation of their memorial, the President let the six American Friends see something of his difficulty. He agreed, of course, that slavery was wrong, but the practical question was the method of its removal. The main problem, he said, was *enforcement*. So far as he could see, a decree "could not be more binding upon the South than the Constitution, and that cannot be enforced in that part of the country now. Would a proclamation of freedom be any more effective?"[14]

While Lincoln disagreed with the members of the delegation in some details, he evidently respected them and was, consequently, influenced by what they said. In any case he set in action less than a month later the very strategy which these people proposed. Part of the reason why he was drawn to them was that they did not denounce the war. "We have no hesitancy," the Progressive Friends said, "in declaring that the government— measuring it by its constitutional obligations—had no alternative

14. *Collected Works*, V, p. 278.

but to seek to suppress this treasonable outbreak by all the means and forces at its disposal, or else to betray the sacred trusts committed to it by the people; and therefore, throughout this fearful struggle, it has had our sympathy, and desire for its success."[15]

An important feature of the meeting between Lincoln and the Friends delegation was that it called forth one of the clearest statements about the divine vocation that he had made up to that time. This statement indicated in miniature the grand theme which was to receive its full formulation in the Second Inaugural thirty-two months later. In short, by June 20, 1862, the spiritual pattern was already established. The New York *Tribune* of June 21 reported, "The President responded very impressively, saying that he was deeply sensible of his need of Divine assistance. He had sometimes thought that perhaps he might be an instrument in God's hand of accomplishing a great work and he certainly was not unwilling to be. Perhaps, however, God's way of accomplishing the end which the memorialists have in view may be different from theirs. It would be his earnest endeavor, with a firm reliance upon the Divine arm, and seeking light from above, to do his duty in the place to which he had been called." Thus, the essentials of his theological position were already formulated by mid-summer of 1862.

Another element in Lincoln's sudden growth in confidence in this crucial summer was a visit on June 24 to West Point, which included a long and confidential talk with General Winfield Scott. The day at the military academy, conferring with the venerable veteran of 1812, did not lead immediately to military victories, but it did lead to a new decisiveness on the part of the Commander-in-Chief. After that, events proceeded with great speed, many of them bringing added anguish, but not one of

15. *Proceedings* of Progressive Friends, 1862, p. 11.

them producing fundamental uncertainty in the sad-faced leader. On June 26 came the start of the Seven Days' Battles near Richmond, ending in the retreat of Union forces under McClellan. On June 27 the President ordered General John Charles Frémont relieved of his command, because, by freeing the slaves in Missouri, the military man had taken too much into his own hands. "Wendell Phillips, in a speech at New York, denounced the Administration as having no definite purpose in the war, and was interrupted by frantic cheers for Frémont."[16]

On July 1 the President made a call for 300,000 three-year men, convinced by this time that the struggle would be long and that capitulation was out of the question. Already, on June 28, in a letter sent through Secretary William Seward to the Union governors meeting in New York, Lincoln indicated the firmness of his own resolve. "I expect," he said, "to maintain this contest until successful or until I die, or am conquered, or my term expires, or Congress or the country forsakes me."[17]

On Sunday, July 13, riding in a carriage on the way to a funeral in the country near Washington, Lincoln confided to Secretary Welles and Secretary Seward his decision to issue a proclamation. Up to that time he had hesitated, in spite of much pressure, because of his great respect for the Constitution. He could not see how the Constitution could permit interference with practices which were legal in particular states. Now he had come to the momentous conclusion that emancipation could be declared on the ground of military necessity since, as Commander-in-Chief, the Constitution laid upon him the protection of the integrity of the country. An amendment to the Constitution could come later, but military necessity could be appealed to prior to the enactment of such an amendment. This is why the Emancipation

16. Stephenson, *Lincoln*, p. 199.
17. *Collected Works*, V, p. 292.

Proclamation, when issued, freed slaves only in those areas engaged in open rebellion. To go further and to emancipate slaves in the border states would have been unconstitutional, since such action would not have been covered by the war powers of the President.

The famous Proclamation, which the President had for so long contemplated in solitude, was read in its preliminary form to the Cabinet on July 22, 1862. Except for Secretaries Welles and Seward, this came to the Cabinet as a surprise. The President's style, they found, had radically altered. He did not ask for advice, the decision having been made, but he nevertheless received some. Montgomery Blair opposed the Proclamation on the ground that it would cause the Administration the loss of the mid-term elections. It would, he said in a subsequent memorandum, "endanger our power in Congress, and put power in the next House of Representatives in the hands of those opposed to the war, or to our mode of carrying it on." The most helpful suggestion, that of Secretary Seward, concerned the date on which the Proclamation should be publicly announced. Seward proposed that publication be postponed until there was some military success to announce, and this counsel the President immediately accepted as wise. Accordingly, the public announcement was not made until after the Battle of Antietam and the subsequent retreat of Lee's army across the Potomac into Virginia. The Proclamation was made known five days after Antietam, on September 22, and became operative January 1, 1863. Thus ended a year of peculiar turmoil.

There was a curious quality about many of Lincoln's conferences during the two months between July 22 and September 22. The President and those in whom he confided had a secret to keep and it is really surprising that all of them succeeded in doing so. "The President," says Randall, "was under the embarrassing necessity of seeming to be non-commital or even hostile toward a policy upon which he was in fact determined."[18] Lincoln actually had the celebrated document in his desk drawer while various persons were trying to argue him into producing it. This, of course, appealed to Lincoln's keen sense of comedy.

During this period of necessary waiting, Lincoln rose to an unusual height in his answer to an editorial, "The Prayer of Twenty Millions," written by Horace Greeley. The editorial, printed in the New York *Tribune* of August 20, 1862, was addressed to Lincoln and expressed dissatisfaction with the policy which he was pursuing "with regard to the slaves of rebels." That Greeley's attack was offensive in tone did not deter the President from taking it seriously and using the opportunity, thus afforded, to state with new clarity the philosophy which he had come with such personal struggle to espouse. But before he stated his policy, he, with subtle humor, took Greeley's self-righteousness down a peg. Referring to the editorial, he said, "If there be in it any statements, or assumptions of fact, which I may know to be erroneous, I do not, now and here, controvert them. If there be in it any inferences which I may believe to be falsely drawn, I do not, now and here, argue against them. If there be perceptible in it an impatient and dictatorial tone, I waive it in deference to an old friend, whose heart I have always supposed to be right."

Then came Lincoln's matured statement of national policy. "I would," he said, "save the Union. I would save it in the shortest way under the Constitution." While there was no doubt about his "*personal* wish that all men everywhere should be free," he had also an *official* duty. While the official responsibility did not modify the personal wish, it necessarily took precedence over it. This is amazingly unambiguous when we hear Lincoln say it, but only by his inner struggle did he achieve such clarity of thought. Because of this inner development, Lincoln could with a com-

18. J. G. Randall, *Lincoln the President* (New York: Dodd, Mead & Co., 1945), II, p. 156.

plete absence of confusion answer Greeley's judgmental mood
with one which was radically different. "My paramount object
in this struggle is to save the Union and is *not* either to save or
to destroy slavery. If I could save the Union without freeing *any*
slave I would do it, and if I could save it by freeing *all* the slaves
I would do it; and if I could save it by freeing some and leaving
others alone I would also do that." Such a policy was not ap-
plauded by extremists on either side, but the Union was saved!

Only five days after Lincoln's reply to Greeley there began the
Second Battle of Bull Run, a battle which ended as disastrously
for the Union forces as the earlier one on the same field more
than a year before. On August 30 the army commanded by General John Pope was routed. It was after virulent complaints and
a whole series of discouraging events that the "Meditation on the
Divine Will," already reproduced in Chapter 1, was written. "It
was," Hay said later, "penned in the awful sincerity of a perfectly
honest soul trying to bring itself into closer communion with its
Maker."[19]

In the same month in which the Meditation was written, Lincoln conferred with Chicago men representing all denominations, who presented a memorial in favor of national emancipation. The President took seriously the message of his Chicago
visitors when he met with them on September 13, 1862. His
careful answer to them reveals both his determination to follow
God's will, as revealed to him, and also his sense of perplexity
because of the conflicting opinions of devout men. "The subject
presented in the memorial," he responded, "is one upon which
I have thought much for weeks past, and I may even say for
months. I am approached with the most opposite opinions and
advice, equally certain that they represent the Divine will. I am
sure that either the one or the other class is mistaken in that

19. Nicolay and Hay, VI, p. 342.

belief, and perhaps in some respects both. I hope it will not be irreverent for me to say that if it is probable that God would reveal his will to others, on a point so connected with my duty, it might be supposed he would reveal it directly to me; unless I am more deceived in myself than I often am, it is my earnest desire to know the will of Providence in this matter." Then the President added, with emphasis, "And if I can learn what it is I will do it!"[20] The men whom the President faced in this important interview were unaware that in only nine days the emancipation for which they pleaded would be announced.

The Battle of Antietam, September 17, 1862, was far more than a military engagement. The biographer of Jefferson Davis, Hudson Strode, stresses this point even more than most Northern scholars have done. "When Lee," he says, "crossed the Potomac back into Virginia on that September 19, 1862, the curve of the Confederacy's fortunes turned decisively downward. Never again was President Davis to know such golden prospects for independence."[21] Apart from the Emancipation Proclamation, Lincoln could not have won such widespread foreign approval, and apart from Antietam, the Proclamation would not have been issued when it was. "And if Lee," writes Strode, "had been victorious the Emancipation Proclamation would certainly have been postponed and probably never have been issued."[22]

Feeling sure that what transpired on the Maryland battlefield, indecisive as it was in some ways, constituted a signal to go forward, the President rewrote the Proclamation on September 21 and presented it to his Cabinet on September 22. Immediately thereafter it was known to the country and to the world. It did not go as far as one set of extremists wished, and it was de-

20. *Collected Works* V, pp. 419, 420.

21. *Jefferson Davis, Confederate President* (New York: Harcourt, Brace and World, Inc., 1959), pp. 306, 307.

22. Ibid., p. 307.

nounced by others as unjust to slave owners, but it accorded with Lincoln's sense of what was best under the circumstances.

When on September 22, 1862, President Lincoln met with his Cabinet in the scene depicted in Carpenter's painting, he deliberately began the momentous occasion with comic relief. Before making the announcement that was to become common knowledge within a few hours, he read, from a book which Artemus Ward had sent to him, a short chapter entitled "High-Handed Outrage at Utica." By such means the often sorrowful man relaxed both himself and others. He was demonstrating again the thesis propounded by Socrates at the end of Plato's *Symposium*: "the true artist in tragedy was an artist in comedy also."

After the comedy, Lincoln continued with the greatest solemnity, revealing for the first time the connection between his decision and his "solemn vow," which some historians have neglected. "Many," says Professor Wolf, "omit the specific statement of Lincoln about a 'solemn vow before God' and describe instead 'a solemn resolution.' This, however, is to substitute a black and white photograph with blurred focus for the rich colors of a masterpiece. The problem is not one of historical evidence. Few incidents in Lincoln's life are so well documented as this one."[23] The President uttered the solemn words, referring to his document as a *declaration*, thus, by a word, connecting his own thought with the main stream of American experience. Another declaration, that of Independence, which had been issued eighty-six years earlier, provided him with a theme which he now proposed to carry to its logical conclusion.

In a year filled with important decisions and encounters, one event which contributed greatly to the final outcome occurred on Sunday morning, October 26. At that time Lincoln was visited by Eliza Gurney and a few others who sought to share with the

23. *Lincoln's Religion*, pp. 17, 18.

President in the bearing of his burdens. What was originally understood by Lincoln as an ordinary interview turned out to be a genuine time of worship.[24] Even though the publication of the Emancipation Proclamation had already occurred, October was a very dark time. Oliver P. Morton, the wartime Governor of Indiana, wrote to the President, "Another three months like the last six and we are lost—lost."[25]

Eliza Gurney (1801-1881) was the widow of the famous English banker and Quaker minister, Joseph John Gurney. An American by birth, President Lincoln at first took her to be English. She had lived in England, at Earlham Hall, Norwich, until her husband's death, after which she returned to her native land. Like any sensitive person, Mrs. Gurney was deeply wounded by the sorrows of the Civil War and felt especial sympathy for President Lincoln in his position of awesome responsibility. Accordingly, she was led, in October, 1862, to try to pay what she called a "religious visit" to the President, being accompanied on this visit by three other Friends, John M. Whitall, Hannah B. Mott, and James Carey. Not one of these sought anything for himself or herself, and none came either to criticize or to offer unasked advice. Because they came only to give spiritual support to one who sorely needed it, the President responded with unusual warmth. Consequently, he encouraged his visitors to stay much longer than the fifteen minutes originally intended, sharing with them in both silence and prayer.

"It was on the morning of the first day of the week, in a beating rain, that the little party repaired to the White House, where they were at once introduced into the private apartment of President Lincoln. . . . Deep thoughtfulness and intense anxiety marked his countenance, and created involuntary sympathy for

24. This aspect of the gathering is mentioned in *White House Sermons*, with introduction by Richard Nixon (New York: Harper & Row, 1972), p. 214.
25. Quoted in Sandburg, *Abraham Lincoln, The War Years*, I, p. 590.

him in this great national crisis."[26] The participants left a careful account of what occurred. They spoke of "the almost awful silence," which moved the President deeply. He was accustomed to hearing words, many of them boring, but he was not accustomed to group silence. "The tears," we are told, "ran down his cheeks," and when vocal prayer was offered, "he reverently bowed his head." After a time of silence Mrs. Gurney gave what was, in essence, a short sermon, which is reproduced in the Lincoln Papers. At the close of her sermon she knelt "and uttered a short but most beautiful, eloquent and comprehensive prayer that light and wisdom might be shed down from on high, to guide our President." After some further silence Lincoln himself spoke, uttering one of the most revealing messages of his entire career. While he obviously had no notes, and could not have had any advance intimation of what his visitors would say or do, the message turned out to be a remarkably finished one. This was possible because what he said was really a summary of what had been developing in his thought during more than a year of intellectual and spiritual struggle. The "instrument" theme here receives its finest expression.

We are indeed going through a great trial—a fiery trial. In the very responsible position in which I happen to be placed, being a humble instrument in the hands of our Heavenly Father, as I am, and as we all are, to work out his great purposes, I have desired that all my works and acts may be according to his will, and that it might be so, I have sought his aid—but if after endeavoring to do my best in the light which he affords me, I find my efforts fail, I must believe that for some purpose unknown to me, He wills it otherwise. If I had had my way, this war would never have been commenced; if I had been allowed my way this war would have been ended before this, but we find it still continues; and we must believe that He permits it for some wise purpose of His

26. *Memoir and Correspondence of Eliza P. Gurney*, edited by Richard F. Mott (Philadelphia: J. B. Lippincott and Company, 1884), pp. 307, 308.

own, mysterious and unknown to us; and though with our limited understandings we may not be able to comprehend it, yet we cannot but believe, that he who made the world still governs it.[27]

The influence of Eliza Gurney on Lincoln's spiritual development is much more profound than has usually been recognized by Lincoln interpreters. Some biographers do not even mention her! Of especial interest is the fact that President Lincoln asked Mrs. Gurney to write to him, the request being transmitted through Isaac Newton, United States Commissioner of Agriculture. The President did this because he felt the need of spiritual support and had found a person who, without a trace of self-seeking, was able to give it. Accordingly, Mrs. Gurney wrote on August 18, 1863, from her new home at Atlantic City. The President's letter of September 4, 1864, which we have already quoted, was his response. In this it is important to remember he referred gratefully to the shared worship in the White House. "I have not forgotten—probably never shall forget—," he wrote, "the very impressive occasion when yourself and friends visited me on a Sabbath forenoon two years ago."

The Lincoln-Gurney letters,[28] taken along with the "Meditation on the Divine Will," provide a genuine introduction to the theme completed in the Second Inaugural. The organ tones of that utterance are already suggested in Lincoln's letter to Mrs. Gurney, especially in the sentence, "The purposes of the Almighty are perfect, and must prevail, though we erring mortals may fail to accurately perceive them in advance." The expressions of the Second Inaugural would not have seemed novel to hearers if they had been able to read in advance the letters which passed between the struggling President and the widow of Joseph John Gurney. Most notable of all in Lincoln's letter is the

27. *Collected Works*, V, p. 478.
28. The entire Lincoln-Gurney correspondence is available in the Library of Congress.

near-perfect style of the sentence, "Surely He intends some great good to follow this mighty convulsion which no mortal could make, and no mortal could stay."

However long we face it, the miracle of Lincoln never ceases to astound us. How can it be that a person devoid of the advantages of a formal education should achieve such perfection of written and spoken style? As was true at Gettysburg, however memorable the deeds may have been, the words were more memorable still. When Lincoln said "The world will little note, nor long remember, what we say here, but it can never forget what they did here," he was being gloriously inaccurate.

The dark and gloomy year, called 1862, turned out to be a year of genuine accomplishment. It was the year in which the Emancipation Proclamation received laborious thought and final publication, going into effect on the first day of 1863. After that there were more months of discouragement, but the big change had already come, because the basic philosophy of Union had at last been formulated. Above all, Lincoln had completely outmaneuvered the troublesome radicals. Many of these, putting their entire emphasis upon the elimination of slavery, had neglected the need to preserve the Union. By making the Emancipation Proclamation a war measure, and not merely one of detached idealism, Lincoln spiked the guns of his severest critics. The war measure as declared was of limited application, but it was hailed by the Abolitionists as good news, and no one could doubt that, with one condition, slavery was doomed in the entire nation. That condition, as Lincoln shrewdly saw, was the successful completion of the war, with the consequent restoration of the Union as a single country. The practical consequence of this action was that nothing that threatened to limit the efficiency of the President, as Commander-in-Chief, had the slightest chance of gaining Abolitionist support.

The sharp tension between the effort to restore the Union and the effort to abolish slavery was something which Reinhold Niebuhr found enduringly intriguing. It was largely because of the way in which Lincoln handled this tension that Professor Niebuhr asserted the eminence of Lincoln as a theologian. "It was significant," Niebuhr said in his West Lectures at Stanford University, "that though Lincoln was prepared to save the union 'half slave and half free' it soon became apparent that this could not be done. The union could be saved only by abolishing slavery. This is a nice symbol of the fact that order precedes justice in the strategy of government; but that only an order which implicates justice can achieve a stable peace. An unjust order quickly invites the resentment and rebellion which lead to its undoing."[29]

It is fortunate that the leader of the nation in its time of greatest internal division was a thinker as well as a politician. As the agonizing months wore on, he saw, increasingly, that there could not be a merely military solution of the conflict. Union was one idea and emancipation was another, but he came to see the intricacy with which these two conceptions were intertwined. The way in which the Emancipation Proclamation was originated, developed, and superbly timed, far from being accidental, was the product of reasoning concerning both order and justice.

The real climax of the year of decision came one month before 1862 was ended, in Lincoln's Message to Congress. In this utterance there appears the true character of the final plateau. "And while," Lincoln began, "it has not pleased the Almighty to bless us with a return of peace, we can but press on guided by the best light He gives us." This was not calm after the storm; it was calm in the midst of storm.

29. *The Children of Light and the Children of Darkness* (New York: Charles Scribner's Sons, 1944), p. 181.

3
Lincoln and the Bible

Nothing short of infinite wisdom could by any possibility have devised and given to man this excellent and perfect moral code.

ABRAHAM LINCOLN

In the Fisk University Library, Nashville, Tennessee, is a copy of the Bible inscribed as follows: "To Abraham Lincoln, President of the United States, the Friend of Universal Freedom, from the Loyal Colored People of Baltimore, as a token of respect and Gratitude. Baltimore, 4th July 1864." The actual presentation of the Bible was made in Washington, September 7, 1864, the donors employing a memorable phrase as they presented the handsome Bible. "Since our incorporation into the American family," they said, "we have been true and loyal." Lincoln's response to this moving presentation afforded him the best opportunity he had ever had to state *clearly* his respect for the Holy Scriptures. "In regard to this Great book," he replied, "I have but to say, it is the best gift God has given to man." Then, as though seizing the opportunity to make his meaning even more clear, he concluded, "All the good Savior gave to the world was communicated through this book. But for it we could not know right from wrong. All things most desirable for man's welfare, here and hereafter, are to be found portrayed in it. To you I return my most sincere thanks for the elegant copy of the great Book of God which you present."[1]

Even a cursory study of Lincoln's speaking style makes the sensitive reader aware of the numerous ways in which the Bible influenced his style, both spoken and written. The Old Testament influence in this regard was greater than that of the Gospels and Epistles or any other part of the New Testament. Especially evident is the parallelism which characterized Hebrew poetry. A good example of such parallelism is the following from the Proclamation of the first Federal Thanksgiving: "No human counsel hath devised nor hath any mortal hand worked out these great things."[2] Another illustration, already provided by the meeting with Mrs. Gurney, is: "If I had had my way, this war would never have been commenced; If I had been allowed my way this war would have ended before this."

The careful reader of the Gettysburg Address cannot fail to note the use of monosyllables, comparable to that exhibited by the Authorized Version, particularly in the Psalms. Of the 265 words in the Gettysburg Address 194 are of one syllable. Similarly, the Twenty-third Psalm, which Lincoln could repeat from memory, has 118 words in all, 92 of these being of one syllable. There is no reason to suppose that the similarity in style was produced by intent nor that Lincoln engaged consciously in imitation. Instead, the Biblical language was so deeply embedded in the great man's mind that it became his normal way of speaking. One of the first to see this clearly was Bishop Matthew Simpson, who gave the funeral oration at Springfield. "He read few books," said Simpson, "but mastered all he read. It was these few,

1. *Collected Works*, VII, pp. 542, 543.
2. *Collected Works*, VI, p. 496.

of which the Bible was chief, which gave the bias to his character, and which partly moulded his style."

While it is generally recognized that young Lincoln heard many passages from the Bible both in his cabin home and in the Baptist meeting house, it is not equally known that he also encountered it in his fragmentary schooling. In this, as in so many aspects of his development, our most reliable evidence is that provided by the man himself. One day in the White House, as the President was speaking to Senator John B. Henderson, he was suddenly reminded of his early education. "Henderson," he asked, "did you ever attend an old blab school? Yes? Well, so did I, and what little schooling I got in early life was in that way. I attended such a school in a log schoolhouse in Indiana where we had no reading books or grammars, and all our reading was done from the Bible. We stood in a long line and read in turn from it." Thus, Lincoln read the Bible and heard it read before his father could afford to own a copy. According to his kinsman, Dennis Hanks, a family Bible was not purchased until 1819, when Abraham was ten years old.[3]

Carl Sandburg pointed out that before Lincoln had "learned to read as a boy, he had heard his mother saying over certain Bible verses day by day as she worked. He had learned these verses by heart; the tones of his mother's voice were in them; and sometimes, as he read these verses, he seemed to hear the voice of Nancy Hanks speaking them." How well he knew some of the verses is shown by the lawyer's response when he drove out into the country to make a will for a woman who was dying. After the will had been signed and witnessed, the woman asked Lincoln to read a few verses out of the Bible. A copy of the Scriptures was produced, but Lincoln did not open it. Instead, he recited

3. The Lincoln family Bible is now exhibited at the Visitors' Center near the birthplace, Hodgenville, Kentucky. See Albert J. Beveridge, *Abraham Lincoln*, I (Boston: Houghton Mifflin Co., 1928), p. 70.

from memory the Twenty-third Psalm and the opening verses of the fourteenth chapter of John.[4]

Biblical references appeared in Lincoln's speeches in a variety of ways. Sometimes the reference was mildly humorous, as when he said, on October 15, 1858, "The Bible says somewhere that we are desperately selfish. I think we would have discovered that fact without the Bible."[5] In short, he had acquired enough theological sophistication to understand that the essence of sin is self-centeredness, and that this is so pervasive that it can enter into all human undertakings, even idealistic and specifically religious ones. He was conscious of the ideological taint of self-interest that corrupts the decisions even of good men. He understood the temptation to self-righteousness which assails the moral crusader.

Frequently, Lincoln employed a verse from the Bible to clinch a point. He had been importuned to make a statement saying that he would not interfere with slaves or slavery in states where they were acceptable. "I have," he wrote to William S. Speer of Tennessee, "done this many, many times; and it is in print, and open to all who will read. Those who will not read or heed what I have already publicly said would not read or heed a repetition of it. If they hear not Moses and the prophets, neither will they be persuaded though one rose from the dead."[6]

An example of the way in which the President could combine his love of humor and the love of the Bible, with consequent devastating effect, is his reaction to the convention which met at Cleveland in 1864 to support Frémont as a challenger to Lincoln's reelection. The convention turned out to be a feeble affair, with practically no accomplishment except the organization of a political party having a single main objective, "the defeat of the

4. Sandburg, *Abraham Lincoln, The Prairie Years*, I, p. 416.
5. *Collected Works*, III, p. 310.
6. Nicolay and Hay, III, pp. 276, 277. The Biblical reference is Luke 16:31.

Lincoln Administration." Attenders met on May 31, 1864, eight days earlier than the Republicans, in order to be able to notify the Convention that it must not nominate Abraham Lincoln for President. The Cleveland preconvention was announced with fanfare and the confident prediction that thousands would attend. When the President was told, finally, that only 400 actually attended, the number immediately triggered in his well-stored mind a humorous Biblical parallel. Refusing to take the challenge seriously, Lincoln compared the Cleveland gathering with that at the Cave of Adullam, mentioned in I Samuel 22:2, where there was a similar number of discontents. "And every one that was in distress, and every one that was in debt, and every one that was discontented, gathered themselves unto him; and he became a captain over them: and there were with him about four hundred men."

Part of Lincoln's humor consisted of quoting Scripture in spirited repartee. This he could do because the Bible is sufficiently varied to balance one statement with another, and Lincoln was so familiar with it that he knew, without hunting, how to pull out the appropriate phrase. When Hugh McCulloch, an official of the Treasury Department, introduced a delegation of New York bankers deferentially, he spoke of their patriotism and quoted, in conclusion, what he thought was a suitable text: "Where the treasure is, there will the heart be also." Reacting quickly to this fatuous use of Scripture, Lincoln without hesitation replied, "There is another text, Mr. McCulloch, which might apply, 'Where the carcass is, there will the eagles be gathered together.'" The President did not need to say that he was quoting Matthew 24:28 and Luke 17:37, and he certainly did not have to hunt for these passages. They were part of the richness of his spiritual resources upon which he could call whenever he needed them.

New light on Lincoln's use of the Bible is now afforded us in the discovery in 1957 of a devotional book made up of select Biblical passages, which was owned and used by Lincoln. It is called *The Believer's Daily Treasure; or, Texts of Scripture Arranged for Every Day in the Year*. This book was first published in 1852, the year that Lincoln began to share regularly in Sunday worship and Mrs. Lincoln joined the church of which Dr. James Smith was pastor. We know something of the way Lincoln valued this volume when we remember that he seldom wrote his name in books he owned, but did write his name in this one. The selections reveal no denominational slant, but represent basic Christianity pointed to the enrichment of daily life. One evident reason why Lincoln appreciated the volume is that it includes much from the Psalms. In a letter to Mrs. Rebecca R. Pomeroy, nurse at the White House, the President wrote, regarding the Psalms, "They are the best, for I find in them something for every day in the week."

The fact that Lincoln could combine humor with his use of the Bible prepares us for the further fact that he did not feel the need to be literalistic in application. His rationalism was so deeply embedded in his character that he tried to interpret the Scriptures intelligently and in the light of accumulated human experience. To the Chicago clergymen who visited Lincoln in the White House prior to the public announcement of the Emancipation Proclamation, the President showed how, with all his faith, it was necessary that he employ all the intelligence he could muster. His visitors, having been given opportunity to state the case for emancipation more fully, pointed out to the President "that he could not deny that the Bible denounced oppression as one of the highest of crimes." Lincoln's response was that the matter was highly complex, that it could not be decided merely by an appeal to authority, and that, consequently, hard thinking was required. "I suppose it will be granted," he said, "that I am not to expect a direct revelation. I must study the plain physical facts of the case, ascertain what is possible and learn what appears to be wise and right."

A good example of the rational approach concerns the text on perfection from the Sermon on the Mount (Matthew 5:48). In a long speech delivered at Chicago on July 10, 1858, as part of the Lincoln-Douglas Debates, Lincoln sought to interpret the meaning of what is widely recognized as a difficult text. "My friend," he began, "has said to me that I am a poor hand to quote Scripture. I will try it again, however. It is said in one of the admonitions of the Lord, 'As your Father in Heaven is perfect, be ye also perfect.' The Savior, I suppose, did not expect that any human creature could be perfect as the Father in Heaven. . . . He set that up as a standard, and he who did most toward reaching that standard, attained the highest degree of moral perfection. So I say in relation to the principle that all men are created equal, let it be as nearly reached as we can. If we cannot give freedom to every creature, let us do nothing that will impose slavery upon any other creature."[7]

Lincoln's study of the Bible and of human life had taught him the practical value of operating in the realm of the possible. He saw the glaring flaw in the reasoning of those who, when they recognize that they cannot do everything, make the absurd conclusion that they will not do anything. He was keenly aware of the way in which perfectionism, wrongly conceived, cuts the nerve of all moral effort. He saw that the "ideal best" is frequently the enemy of the "concrete good," especially in the political realm. Freely cognizant that neither he nor his colleagues could at that time eliminate slavery where it was entrenched, he nevertheless determined to do what he could, viz., to oppose its extension. Here was the fundamental issue which divided him and Senator Douglas, as the latter argued for the possibility of

7. *Collected Works*, II, 501.

extension under the doctrine of popular or "squatter" sovereignty.

It is important to remember that, partly in response to the pioneer culture in which he was steeped, Abraham Lincoln's religion was centered far more in the Bible than in the Church. William J. Wolf's recognition of this fact is vital to his understanding of Lincoln's religion. He makes the point more than once that for Lincoln "the Bible rather than the Church remained the highroad to the knowledge of God."[8] The great man's attitude to the Bible is indicated far more by the way in which he used it than by what he said about it. His method is not literalistic, and certainly he was not collecting proof texts to support his own pet opinions, but he was always reverent in his many references. A good example of reverent use is the well-known passage in the Second Inaugural, "let us judge not that we be not judged." Often, as in this case, he upheld the self-respect of his hearers by assuming that they were as familiar with the noble passages as he himself was. In referring to the two contesting sides in the terrible war he said, "Both read the same Bible."

The long train journey from Springfield to Washington gave the President-elect numerous opportunities to clarify his position by the use of Biblical references. Thus, in Indianapolis on February 11, 1861, he replied to Governor Morton and other citizens by saying, "When the people rise in masses in behalf of the Union and the liberties of their country, truly may it be said, 'The gates of hell shall not prevail against them.' "[9] It would have been indelicate for the speaker to say that he was quoting Matthew 16:18, applying to the Union the words which Christ had applied to the Church. In a similar fashion, at Independence Hall, Philadelphia, on February 21, 1861, Lincoln said, in refer-

8. *Lincoln's Religion*, p. 75. The July 1, 1964, issue of *Presbyterian Life* features a careful article by Professor Wolf, "Lincoln and the Bible."
9. *Collected Works*, IV, pp. 193, 194.

ence to the ideas involved in the Declaration of Independence and the Constitution of the United States, "May my right hand forget its cunning and my tongue cleave to the roof of my mouth if ever I prove false to those teachings."[10] He did not need to say that he was employing, in a new connection, the words of Psalm 137:5 and 6. "America," by implication, was a substitute for "Jerusalem."

Often, in both Lincoln's private letters and his public addresses, the Biblical influence was oblique and subtle. Parts of phrases would appear without specific and overt reference. Thus, in a letter written to Ward Hill Lamon on June 11, 1858, he wrote, "As to the inclination of some Republicans to favor Douglas that is one of the chances I have to run, and which I intend to run with patience."[11] The writer obviously knew by heart the beginning of the twelfth chapter of Hebrews. That he could combine the Old Testament with the New is indicated by the way in which, in the famous "House Divided" speech, he used the words of Ecclesiastes 9:4 about the superiority of a living dog over a dead lion.[12] In this, as was his custom, Lincoln did not say what the reference was; it was sufficient that he knew and that many of his hearers knew. Lincoln was experiencing one of his magnificent bursts of vitality in the summer when he was forty-nine years old, and he was in great form.

The "House Divided" theme is the most illustrious example of Lincoln's use of the Bible in a public address, the theme sticking in the public mind because it was so pertinent to the contemporary situation. By this teaching device, the speaker's point was made far more memorable. The address was delivered at Springfield, Illinois, on June 16, 1858, at the close of the Republican state convention. It was this convention which nominated Abraham

10. Ibid., p. 239.
11. *Collected Works*, II, p. 459.
12. Ibid., p. 467.

Lincoln as their candidate for the United States Senate and which led to the contest in which Lincoln was defeated by Senator Douglas. The address did much to bring the hitherto obscure lawyer to national attention. "If we could first know *where* we are," the speaker began, "and *whither* we are tending, we could then better judge *what* to do, and *how* to do it." These opening words were soon repeated and are widely used to this day, but it is doubtful if their impact would have been as great without the Biblical connection which followed so aptly.

In answering the question of where the country then stood, Lincoln found that it was best to tell the sorrowful truth and to admit that the nation was divided. To make this truth vivid he turned to the words found in all three of the Synoptic Gospels (Matthew 12:25, Mark 3:25, Luke 11:17). His reference, put in quotation marks in his Springfield address, is closer to the Marcan version than to any other. "A house divided against itself," he quoted, "cannot stand." Immediately he made the American application, "I believe this government cannot endure, permanently half *slave* and half *free*." He hastened to say that in spite of the anguish the division was temporary, and that failure was by no means inevitable. With remarkable clarity he added to his warning, "I do not expect the Union to be *dissolved*—I do not expect the house to fall—but I do expect it will cease to be divided."[13] Here was illustrated something of his genius in both style and content.

Though the "House Divided" theme is popularly associated with the nominating convention of June, 1858, this was neither the first nor the last use of the reference in Lincoln's public life. He had already employed the theme a month earlier in an address at Edwardsville, Illinois, when he expressed dismay at the way in which churches as well as political bodies were dividing. Divi-

13. Ibid., p. 461.

sion seemed to be the order of the day, and this he deeply deplored. When Lincoln first made public the "House Divided" theme, it was already an old one in his own mind. This is indicated by what he said at Edwardsville. After stating, as he was to do later, the impossibility of divided endurance, he said, "I expressed this belief a year ago."[14] Later, in an address delivered at Columbus, Ohio, on September 16, 1859, the idea was repeated almost verbatim.[15]

Lincoln's acquaintance with the Scriptures, though well established in early youth when few books were available to him, increased during his mature life. He adopted at several stages of his career the practice of daily Bible reading. One evidence of this practice, to which reference has already been made, came in the crisis of 1841 when Mrs. Speed gave Lincoln a Bible.

An important insight into Lincoln's character is the way in which he valued the printed word. This comes out vividly in his ambitious address, "Discoveries and Inventions." On April 6, 1858, he delivered this before the Young Men's Association of Bloomington, Illinois, and later, in a completely rewritten form, at Illinois College, at Decatur, and finally at Springfield. In this nonpolitical address Lincoln expressed the conviction that the written word was "the great invention of the world." It was the great invention, he concluded, because it liberates mankind from the bondage of both the present and the local. "When writing was invented," he said, "any important observation, likely to lead to a discovery, had at least a chance of being written down, and, consequently, a better chance of never being forgotten."[16] It was in such terms as these that he valued the Scriptures so highly. He saw how intellectually and spiritually impoverished a person would be if he were limited to his own personal resources. The

14. Ibid., p. 452.
15. *Collected Works*, III, p. 407.
16. Ibid., p. 362.

Bible, he recognized, vastly enlarged the area of experience on which an individual might depend. In this regard we learn even more from Lincoln's practice than from any stated doctrine. The Lecture on Inventions contains thirty-four separate references to the Bible.

Of all of Lincoln's affirmations indicating his deep dependence on the Biblical revelation none is more impressive than that made to his long-time friend, Joshua Speed, in the summer of 1864. Lincoln used the Soldier's Home, on the north edge of the District of Columbia, as a summer refuge from the heat of the Potomac Valley, riding there many evenings and sleeping there. One evening he was visited in his room by Joshua Speed of Kentucky. Speed had shared his room with Lincoln when the newcomer first settled in Springfield in 1837 and was the one to whom the developing Lincoln had confided intimately concerning his own intellectual and emotional struggles. In a lecture prepared by Speed, the doubts of Lincoln's early life were frankly recognized. Then came a passage which tells the modern reader a great deal.

The only evidence I have of any change, was in the summer before he was killed. I was invited out to the Soldier's Home to spend the night. As I entered the room, near night, he was sitting near a window intently reading his Bible. Approaching him, I said, "I am glad to see you so profitably engaged." "Yes," said he, "I am profitably engaged." "Well," said I, "if you have recovered from your skepticism, I am sorry to say that I have not." Looking me earnestly in the face, and placing his hand on my shoulder, he said, "You are wrong, Speed; take all of this Book upon reason that you can, and the balance on faith, and you will live and die a happier man."[17]

The President's words to his friend Speed are especially significant because Speed was not one of the many who were trying to make a case for Lincoln's religious orthodoxy. Indeed, he was

17. Speed, *Lecture on Abraham Lincoln*, pp. 32–33.

on the other side though not, of course, as extreme as Herndon. We must remember that Speed sold his store and went back to Kentucky twenty years before Lincoln's departure from Springfield, so that apart from letters and occasional visits Speed had little opportunity of knowing very much about the spiritual growth which his friend was experiencing. For example, he did not know except at second hand the significant influence of Dr. James Smith, the Scottish pastor of the First Presbyterian Church of Springfield. Scant attention has been given to the fact that soon after his wife's admission to the church, Lincoln gave a lecture on the Bible in the church building upon the invitation of the Session. The lecture was sponsored not only by the First Presbyterian Church, but also by the Bible Society of Springfield, Lincoln's local popularity assuring a full house. Thoughtful people reported that the lawyer presented the ablest defense of the Bible ever heard from that particular pulpit.

We wish, of course, that we could read Lincoln's lecture on the Bible, but we do not have it. We do, however, have something of genuine value in Dr. Smith's statement, which appears to be a synopsis of Lincoln's argument. Lincoln's conclusion, as reported by his pastor, was an early example of his speaking style which later became familiar. Part of this is the epigraph of the present chapter. "It seems to me," he said, "that nothing short of infinite wisdom could by any possibility have devised and given to man this excellent and perfect moral code. It is suited to men in all the conditions of life, and inculcates all the duties they owe to their Creator, to themselves, and to their fellow men."[18]

The Lecture on the Bible was clearly influenced by the reasoning of Dr. Smith. That Lincoln held the Springfield pastor in high esteem is shown by the fact that their friendship continued to the end, and that during Lincoln's presidency, Smith was

18. Letter of December 24, 1872, from James Smith to William Herndon. This was first published in *Daily Illinois Journal*, March 12, 1867.

made consul at Dundee in his native Scotland. On January 9, 1863, Lincoln wrote in a note to Secretary Seward, "Dr. Smith, mentioned within, is an intimate personal friend of mine."[19] Lincoln's nomination of James Smith for the consulship was confirmed by the Senate on February 18, 1863. That Dr. Smith had an enduring effect on Lincoln's mature thinking there is no doubt. Part of the reason for the mutual admiration of these two men is that the Scotsman, like Lincoln, had been a doubter. Lincoln's first serious contact with Smith's mind came during a visit to Kentucky in 1849, when Lincoln picked up Smith's book, *The Christian's Defense.*

There is much evidence of the impact of Smith's book on Lincoln's mind. Witnesses to this were John T. Stuart, the early law partner, and Lincoln's brother-in-law, Ninian W. Edwards. "I have been reading a work of Dr. Smith on the evidences of Christianity," Lincoln told Edwards, "and have heard him preach and converse on the subject and am now convinced of the truth of the Christian religion."[20] Lincoln admitted that his views had been modified, and even went so far as to declare that Smith's argument was "unanswerable."

As he examined the Bible carefully under Dr. Smith's tutelage, Lincoln looked at the entire Biblical record as a lawyer, who, eager to find the truth, investigates testimony. The Scotsman was naturally familiar with the argument of David Hume and answered Hume in a spirit similar to that of Dr. Samuel Johnson. He provided Lincoln with what, to a lawyer, was a wholly congenial approach. The familiar Johnson statement, made in Boswell's presence soon after their first meeting, was, "The Christian religion has very strong evidences. It, indeed, appears in some degree strange to reason; but in History we have undoubted

19. *Collected Works,* VI, p. 51.
20. See William E. Barton, *The Soul of Abraham Lincoln* (New York: George H. Doran Company, 1920), p. 164.

facts, against which, in reasoning *à priori*, we have more arguments than we have for them: but then, testimony has great weight, and casts the balance." This was precisely the kind of thinking to which Lincoln was introduced by the pastor of the First Presbyterian Church of Springfield.

Lincoln's greatest interest in the Bible, and the spur to his steady reading of it, was the hope of finding light on the social and political problems which faced the nation. He was looking for light and by his perusal of the Scriptures he hoped he might find it. This was vastly more important than any effect upon his personal piety. Though he did not admire preachers who used their pulpits for political pronouncements, he saw the Biblical faith as something which influenced his own political decisions. God, he believed, was directing the social order through finite individuals who were His instruments.

Lincoln was drawn to the Bible partly because it deals so largely with events. The divine Ruler is seen throughout both the Old and New Testaments as the God of history. The chief way, Lincoln saw, in which God's will is revealed is not in abstract ideas, but in the development of the story of man's struggles, particularly his struggle to be free. The Israelites *did* become liberated from Egyptian bondage; they *did* occupy the promised land; they *did* prepare the way for the coming of Christ; the infant Christian fellowship *did* survive. As Lincoln advanced in his religious thinking he put greater and greater emphasis, not upon the details, but upon the magnitude of the historical unfolding. Whatever criticism might be made of his faith, it could not be truly said that his God was too small. God, as the Bible revealed Him, seemed to Lincoln to be One who dealt not merely with isolated individuals for whom He cares, but for liberty and justice for the entire human race. His fundamental affinity was with the prophetic strain.

The magnitude of Lincoln's theology becomes evident when

we recognize the degree to which he transcended the popular polarization of piety versus political action. The clear conclusion from his own words was that he was not willing to settle for either of these in isolation. He could not abide the kind of religion which made a man interested only in the salvation of his own soul without any reference to human injustice, such as that of slavery. His belief in God and his agonizing search for God's will had implications for the ways in which men live with and treat their fellow men. On the other hand, he had no admiration for the person whose religion was political and nothing more. His theology led him to say "and" rather than "or" when he faced the complexity of the Gospel. He was concerned about wider issues than personal comfort, yet he saw that the Gospel *does* provide personal comfort for the distraught individual. As we have already seen, Lincoln reminded his own father, as he lay dying, that God's eye is on the sparrow.

It was in connection with the institution of slavery that Lincoln's experience of the Bible made the greatest single difference, and in which the complexity of the problem became most apparent. He had to face the fact that the Bible does not contain a single overt condemnation of human slavery. If Lincoln had not known this in any other way he was bound to be faced with the fact through the insistence of proslavery advocates. We know, for example, that he was familiar with the ideas of the Reverend Frederick A. Ross, author of *Slavery Ordained of God* (Philadelphia, 1857). In a fragment on proslavery theology, which may have been produced October 1, 1858,[21] Lincoln mentioned Dr. Ross and lampooned his position. The basic question, Lincoln recognized, is not whether we should follow the will of God, but what the will of God really is. Does God will that the slave should be free? Lincoln was sufficiently honest to admit that the Bible

21. Nicolay and Hay assign this date. See *Collected Works*, III, pp. 204, 205.

provides no explicit answer to this question. He was well aware that the Hebrew patriarchs owned slaves and that when slavery is mentioned, even in the New Testament, it is not clearly condemned. In fact, the slave is enjoined to be obedient to his earthly master (Ephesians 6:5). Thus Lincoln was forced to admit that when we look for a simple answer about God's will in this particular, "his revelation—the Bible—gives none—or, at most, none but such as admits of a squabble, as to its meaning."

Lincoln's appeal to the Bible on the question of slavery sought an answer below the surface. While the Bible does not directly condemn slavery, he saw that it does stress both justice and mercy and moves toward an emphasis upon helping any who are in need. He summarized the Christian "rule of charity" as "Give to him that is needy." This is evidently based on Christ's words, "Verily I say unto you, Inasmuch as ye have done it unto one of the least of these my brethren, ye have done it unto me" (Matthew 25:40). The same conception is expressed by the parable of the Good Samaritan which teaches that my neighbor is the one who needs me (Luke 10:29–37). The practical answer to slavery, Lincoln thought, starts with compassion, which was, he held, intrinsic to the Biblical message.

On a still deeper level, Lincoln saw that the Biblical revelation really undermines slavery by its conception of the nature of man. The first strong indication that this line of thought would be followed by Lincoln came in a little noticed address given at Lewistown, Illinois, August 17, 1858. Early in his two-and-a-half-hour speech, the relatively unknown Lincoln called attention to the ethical neutralism of his famous adversary. Referring specifically to slavery, he said that "to Judge Douglas belongs the *distinction* of having never said that he regarded it either as an evil or a good, morally right or morally wrong." The heart of Lincoln's argument was an appeal to the deeper meaning of the Declaration of Independence. Speaking of the thirteen original colonies, he said, "These communities, by their representatives in old Independence Hall, said to the whole world of men: 'We hold these truths to be self evident: that all men are created equal; that they are endowed by their Creator with certain unalienable rights; that among these are life, liberty and the pursuit of happiness.' This was their majestic interpretation of the economy of the Universe. This was their lofty and wise, and noble understanding of the justice of the Creator to His creatures. [Applause.] Yes, gentlemen, to *all* His creatures, to the whole great family of man. In their enlightened belief, nothing stamped with the Divine image and likeness was sent into the world to be trodden on, and degraded, and imbruted by its fellows. They grasped not only the whole race of man then living, but they reached forward and seized upon the farthest posterity. They erected a beacon to guide their children and their children's children, and the countless myriads who should inhabit the earth in other ages."[22]

In this address, fortunately preserved in part by the Chicago *Press and Tribune*, August 21, 1858, we come very near to the heart of Lincoln's theology as it applies to human betterment. Here we are far removed from sectarian competition or from emphasis upon the presence or absence of proof texts regarding slavery or any other human practice. Lincoln, in marked contrast to most of his contemporaries, reached back to the very roots of the faith which sustained him. Central to everything else was the conviction that the dignity of man is *derivative*. Man's glory lies not, Lincoln thought, in his goodness, for this is often nonexistent. He derives glory, instead, from his being made in the image of the Living God. Poring over the Scriptures, Lincoln had found his clue in the very first chapter: "God created man in his own image, in the image of God created he him" (Genesis 1:27). It followed that no person, of whatever color or nationality, was a

22. *Collected Works*, II, p. 546.

mere thing to be bought and sold. Here is perhaps the most revolutionary idea in the world because, if it were ever truly followed, it would overcome all barriers to human development.

The debate between Douglas and Lincoln in the summer and autumn of 1858 was bound to include some aspects that were unlovely. Judge Douglas thought, for example, that he had a good opportunity to attack Lincoln at a vulnerable point by accusing him of encouraging the intermarriage of the races. If he could have made this stick he would have dealt Lincoln a severe blow. The people, generally, were opposed to racial intermarriage. The Judge's argument was not that Lincoln had openly advocated the mixing of the races, since he had not done so, but that this was where Lincoln's position would necessarily lead.

Lincoln had thought upon this subject too long to be caught in the trap which his opponent sought to set. "I protest, now and forever," countered Lincoln, "against that counterfeit logic which presumes that because I do not want a negro woman for a slave, I do, necessarily, want her for a wife." Lincoln, grounded as he was in the Biblical conception of equal justice, kept the emphasis there, and refused to be drawn into questions which were extraneous to the basic issue. "There are white men enough to marry all the white women," he said, "and enough black men to marry all the black women, and in God's name, let them be so married."[23]

The Judge, who claimed to respect the Declaration of Independence as truly as Lincoln did, interpreted its key propositions in a different manner. He pointed out, as Lincoln had already admitted, that the Founding Fathers did not abolish slavery. And why not? Was it because when they said "all men," they meant "all white men"? Lincoln's repudiation of this narrowed interpretation illustrates clearly an important feature of his own polit-

23. *Collected Works*, II, p. 498. See also p. 405.

ical philosophy: in moral decisions human beings choose positions which are less than perfect, because the only available alternatives are worse.

Lincoln's acceptance of the philosophical conception of comparative evils is so crucial that it requires elaboration. It was their failure to appreciate this sophisticated idea which actuated many of his harshest critics in his own generation, as it activates many critics even now. The crucial idea is that moral decisions are always made in the light of alternatives. Because all positions have something wrong with them, the task of the good person is to choose the least damaging among those that are possible. It is wrong to pull up the tares if, in so doing, we pull up the wheat also (Matthew 13:29); it is wrong to eradicate a particular evil practice if, in doing so, we create another harm which outweighs the good. One of Lincoln's illustrations of this principle was drawn from the life of Henry Clay whose eulogy he gave on July 6, 1852, in the Illinois Hall of Representatives. "Cast into life where slavery was already widely spread and deeply seated, he did not perceive, as I think no wise man has perceived, how it could be at *once* eradicated, without producing a greater evil, even to the cause of human liberty itself."[24] Lincoln was well aware of the delicacy of such an intellectual operation and of the difficulty of weighing comparative evils, but he also saw that there is no escape from this operation, provided we try to live wisely and well.

The framers of the Declaration of Independence, including even Thomas Jefferson, had to face comparative evils. The upshot of the situation, as Lincoln analyzed it, was that an uncompromising stand against existent slavery in 1776 would have had no important effect except that of eliminating the possibility of creating a nation at all. The lesser evil, Lincoln thought as he

24. Ibid., p. 130.

supposed the Founders thought, was that of allowing entrenched slavery for a time in the hope of its ultimate extinction. At this point his study of the thinking of Thomas Jefferson was exceptionally productive.

In the same address in which Lincoln presented the idea of "relative perfection," i.e., the kind which is in the realm of the possible, he was explicit about the choice which the framers of the Declaration were, unfortunately, forced to make. "It may be argued," he said, "that there are certain conditions that make necessities and impose them upon us, and to the extent that a necessity is imposed upon a man he must submit to it. I think that was the condition in which we found ourselves when we established this government. We had slavery among us, we could not get our constitution unless we permitted them to remain in slavery, we could not secure the good we did secure if we grasped for more, and having by necessity submitted to that much, it does not destroy the principle that is the charter of our liberties."[25]

Very few of the words of Abraham Lincoln repay study more than these which were uttered at Chicago on July 10, 1858. Here, in some of the most careful reasoning in which he ever engaged, Lincoln began by realizing that ethics is, and must always be, the science of the possible. Choices are made, not in some ideal or abstract situation, but in the realm of the real. The best, consequently, must always be the best *under the circumstances*, i.e., in the light of actual alternatives. This is why, as Lincoln understood moral philosophy, decisions are never really simple. Since any conceivable choice involves difficulties of its own, a position is accepted not because it is wholly satisfactory, but because there is no better one available.

In loyalty to the Biblical heritage, which meant so much to him, Lincoln was forced to oppose interpreters of the Scriptures

25. Ibid., p. 501.

on both sides of the slavery issue. Just as he rejected the oversimplification of the apologist for slavery who could point out that
the Bible mentions slavery without specific condemnation, so
equally he rejected the oversimplification of the fanatical Abolitionist of the John Brown variety. The problem, as Abraham
Lincoln saw it, had to be faced at a deeper level than any provided
by Biblical literalism. In concentrating upon the profound idea
of the divine image, Lincoln discovered this deeper level.

Much as Lincoln admired Thomas Jefferson, it is important to
see how the sixteenth President differed from the third. Jefferson,
for all his brilliance, was never wholly liberated from his deistic
prejudices. Lincoln, though he willingly accepted the leadership
of Jefferson in political affairs, consciously separated from him in
religious perspective. Consequently, he saw even more clearly
than Jefferson the deep significance of what he called "our national axioms." When Lincoln repeated the phrase, "all men are
created equal," he understood thoroughly that these words need
not imply *factual* equality, which, of course, does not exist. In a
factual sense, people are conspicuously *unequal*. To understand
this we need only to contrast Jefferson's own achievements with
those of his neighbors, white or black. The equality to which our
national axiom refers is not that of talents or of accomplishments.
It is an equality of derivative value, according to which each
person, regardless of color, sex, or status, is precious in God's
estimation because each is His peculiar creation. In short, the
Declaration of Independence makes sense in a theological context, but fails to make sense in any other. It is a mark of Lincoln's
greatness that he saw this so clearly and that he saw it so early.

The contemporary Lincoln scholar who seems to have grasped
the delicate relationship between Jefferson and Lincoln better
than any other is William J. Wolf, who makes the following
observation: "Jefferson was Lincoln's mentor in political philosophy, but Lincoln's religious perspective was more concrete than

Jefferson's. Lincoln went deeper than 'self-evidence' for these truths, even further than the somewhat deistic phrase 'endowed by their Creator.' For Lincoln the Creator was the living God of history, revealed in the Bible, Whose judgments were continuously written on the pages of history and recorded in the human conscience."[26]

Because he was aware of another dimension than that of politics, Lincoln was amazingly liberated from the dangers of idolatry, including the idolatry of the nation. No nation, he held, is wholly sovereign because every nation is under judgment. In his enduring love of the Psalms he was familiar with the words, "the Lord is high above all nations" (113:4). In like fashion, he would not accept the ultimacy of "popular sovereignty" as proposed by Douglas in defense of the extension of slavery to the territories. Douglas had, indeed, fastened upon an axiom, but, since it was not sufficiently basic, it was itself under judgment. It was not even sufficient, Lincoln thought, to appeal to liberty for this may mean many different and even opposite things. In an address at Baltimore in the spring of 1864 the President affirmed that "the world has never had a good definition of liberty." "With some," he continued, "the word liberty may mean for each man to do as he pleases with himself and the product of his labor; while with others the same word may mean for some men to do as they please with other men, and the product of other men's labor."[27]

There is no possibility of understanding Abraham Lincoln if we do not understand how deeply the fundamental teachings of the Bible had entered into his mature mentality. In consequence the astute politician was always more than a political thinker. He was more than a political thinker because he was always appealing to a higher moral code. He believed, as he said at Clinton, Illinois, that the principles for which he struggled would eventu-

26. Wolf, *Lincoln's Religion*, pp. 95, 96.
27. *Collected Works*, VII, pp. 301, 302.

ally prevail, and the reason for his hope was that "there is a just and righteous God in Heaven."[28] In the light of this conviction he concluded his most famous address before election to the Presidency with the memorable words: "Let us have faith that right makes might, and in that faith, let us to the end, dare to do our duty, as we understand it."[29]

28. *Colllected Works*, III, p. 448.
29. Ibid., p. 550.

4
Lincoln at Prayer

I have sought His aid.

ABRAHAM LINCOLN

On October 5, 1818, Nancy Lincoln died. The disease which killed the pioneer mother was known locally as "milk sick." In the late summer and early autumn the hungry cattle were attracted to a plant called white snake root, which grew in shady places in the forest and which produced clusters of chalk-white flowers. When the cows ate enough of the flowers they developed "trembles" and three days later were dead. Humans who drank the milk from these cows were themselves stricken. One of the cows belonging to Thomas Lincoln showed signs of the trembles and soon his neighbor, Thomas Sparrow, died of the disease. Mrs. Sparrow was fatally stricken also, and then Nancy, after she had nursed some of the neighbors, became herself a victim.

Dennis Hanks reported the tragedy as he remembered it.[1] Of

1. The report of Dennis Hanks is in the Herndon-Weik manuscript. The report was made June 13, 1865. Hanks was the adopted son of Thomas Sparrow. For a full account of the sickness and death of Nancy Lincoln see Louis A. Warren, *Lincoln's Youth, Seven to Twenty-one.*

the thirty-six-year-old woman he said, "She knew she was going to die and called up the children to her dying side and told them to be good and kind to their father—to one another and to the world, expressing a hope that they might live as they had been taught by her to live . . . love—reverence and worship God." This scene left a deep impression on Nancy's nine-year-old boy and his older sister, Sarah. Finally, the desperately sick woman spoke directly to her young son, as follows: "I am going away from you, Abraham, and I shall not return. I know that you will be a good boy, that you will be kind to Sarah and to your father. I want you to live as I have taught you, and to love your Heavenly Father."

The sorrowful scene in the Indiana forest was never erased from Abraham Lincoln's memory. Years later, when Willie died in the White House, the grief-stricken President spoke to the nurse, Mrs. Pomeroy, saying: "I had a good Christian mother, and her prayers have followed me thus far through life." In his own practice of prayer, Lincoln thought of himself as maintaining a trust which had been laid upon him by his dying mother. The determination to be faithful to a trust was one of the most prominent features of Lincoln's mature character.

The evidence of Abraham Lincoln's own practice of personal prayer is so abundant that no thoughtful person can deny it. He prayed alone, and he called the nation to prayer; he prayed for guidance, and he prayed in gratitude; he prayed in defeat, and he prayed in victory. Often noted was his reverence when others engaged in vocal prayer.[2] Along with his unashamed reverence, however, went a large measure of reticence. Though Mrs. Pomeroy said that she heard the President praying aloud in the White House, we have no text of any vocal prayer uttered by him. Something of his reticence is indicated by the fact that when he attended with regularity the weekly prayer meeting at the New

2. One report of this is provided in the *Life and Letters of Elizabeth Comstock.*

York Avenue Presbyterian Church in Washington, he elected to sit unseen in the pastor's study with the door ajar. The President told his pastor, Dr. Phineas D. Gurley, that he received important help from these unostentatious gatherings, chiefly because they were characterized more by prayer than by the making of speeches. By this time in his life, with countless heavy burdens upon him, Lincoln had entirely outgrown juvenile delight in religious argument. Talking with God seemed to the mature Lincoln more important than talking *about* Him.

On Sundays at New York Avenue Presbyterian Church, President Lincoln showed his personal respect for vocal prayer by standing during the pastoral prayer, as did a number of other men who were present. William Henry Roberts, Stated Clerk of the Presbyterian General Assembly, reported on Lincoln's attitude in worship. "I was seated," he said, "not far from Mr. Lincoln at Sunday services for a year and a half, and his attitude was always that of an earnest and devout worshiper."

As a supplement to the record provided by outside observers, we have in some instances Lincoln's own account of his practice of prayer. A good example is included in his famous letter to Mrs. Lydia Bixby in which he reported his own personal prayer. "I pray," he wrote, "that our Heavenly Father may assuage the anguish of your bereavement, and leave you only the cherished memory of the loved and lost, and the solemn pride that must be yours, to have laid so costly a sacrifice upon the altar of Freedom."[3] The widow, we now know, had lost only two sons rather than five as originally reported, but this does not alter the appeal of Lincoln's prayerful response. On the whole it is better to trust Lincoln than his reporters. Mrs. Pomeroy could have been mistaken when she said that she had heard the President praying aloud, but the evidence provided by the man himself is dependable.

3. *Collected Works*, VIII, p. 117.

Fortunately, we have the cumulative testimony of many different people converging on a single point, one of these reporters being Lincoln's own wife. She said that on the morning of the first inauguration Lincoln read the conclusion of his address to the assembled family and then, when they had withdrawn from the room, prayed audibly for strength and guidance. Noah Brooks reported that the President, after entering the White House and in spite of the demands of a busy schedule, observed daily the practice of prayer. "Sometimes," said Brooks, "it was only ten words, but those ten words he had." His chief private secretary, John Nicolay, who had a better opportunity than most people to know the truth about Lincoln's personal devotional habits, was unequivocal in his testimony. "Mr. Lincoln," he said, "was a praying man. I know that to be a fact and I have heard him request people to pray for him, which he would never have done had he not believed that prayer is answered. . . . I have heard him say that he prayed."[4]

The conclusion we are bound to reach as we face the accumulated evidence is that Lincoln's piety, though subdued, was genuine and deep. Something of the depth was revealed on the way to the burial of Willie, when the President said, "I will try to go to God with my sorrows." The national leader on his knees was a model vividly presented to Lincoln in his early boyhood when he read Weems' *Life of Washington*, and learned the story of how Isaac Potts found General Washington praying at Valley Forge in the winter of 1777. Present-day visitors to the National Cathedral in Washington are sometimes reminded of the scene in the woods near Valley Forge when they study the statue of Lincoln kneeling at prayer. The statue is the creation of the sculptor, Herbert S. Houck, who was influenced by a report of his own grandfather. Whether the scene is historical we do not know. But we do know what Lincoln, perhaps engaging in a figure of

4. For Nicolay's statement see William E. Curtis, *The True Abraham Lincoln*, pp. 385, 386.

speech, confided to his intended secretary, Noah Brooks. "I have," he said, "been driven many times upon my knees by the overwhelming conviction that I had no where else to go."[5]

Our most reliable knowledge of Lincoln's experience of prayer comes from the war years, yet there are many instances of the intensity of his experience of prayer in earlier periods. Thus, on October 30, 1858, as he was concluding his strenuous campaign in the senatorial race against Stephen A. Douglas, he told of his own anguish which had been involved in his decision to try for high office. He said that if the restriction on the extension of slavery could have been retained, he would have remained in private life. The reference to prayer was in connection with this hard personal decision. "God knows," he said, "how sincerely I prayed from the first that this field of ambition might not be opened."[6]

The major change regarding prayer, which came with the awesome responsibility of national leadership, lay not in the fact that he prayed, for this he had done before, but rather that he became able to speak of prayer openly and with an entire absence of embarrassment. Though never flamboyant about it, he was finally able, when the occasion warranted, to speak freely about the deepest experiences of his life.

One of the most humbling yet supporting of the experiences which came to Lincoln was that of knowing that others were praying for him. At the beginning of his most discouraging year, Senator Harlan brought to Lincoln a message from the Quakers of Iowa, to which the President replied on January 5, 1862. "It is," he said, "most cheering and encouraging for me to know that in the efforts which I have made, and am making, for the restoration of a righteous peace to our country, I am upheld and sustained by the good wishes and prayers of God's people."[7]

5. See Noah Brooks, *Harper's Monthly*, July 1865.
6. *Collected Works*, III, p. 334.
7. Nicolay and Hay, VI, p. 327.

It is no surprise to the modern student of Lincoln's thought that he was sophisticated in his theology of prayer. Convinced of the radical contrast between God's wisdom and our own, he did not suppose for a moment that the prayers of a finite person can alter the infinite will. Consequently, his chief form of prayer was that of seeking to know what the will of God really is. Conscious always of his finitude, Lincoln realized that in seeking to know God's will, he might easily be mistaken. In any case he was aware that in the war *somebody* was mistaken. Contradiction is the perfect evidence, he thought, of human fallibility.

Part of Lincoln's realism about the difficulties of prayer arose from his early recognition that many on the other side of the conflict were themselves engaged in prayer. Indeed, he concluded that Southerners were probably praying more earnestly than the people who professed to have Union sympathies. He knew, of course, that the President of the Confederate States was a man of prayer much as he, himself, was. This we know today better than we knew earlier, as a result of Hudson Strode's careful research.

On April 23, 1865, after the war had ended, and Lincoln had been assassinated, Jefferson Davis wrote from Charlotte, North Carolina, to his wife, "I have prayed to our Heavenly Father to give me wisdom and fortitude equal to the demands of the position in which Providence has placed me."[8] Both sides, Lincoln realized, prayed to the same God.

Immediately after his removal to Richmond, President Davis appointed June 13, 1861, as "a day of fasting and prayer throughout the Confederacy." This preceded all of the calls to National Prayer which Lincoln was later to make. At his inauguration at Montgomery, Alabama, Davis ended his address as follows:

8. Strode, *Private Letters of Jefferson Davis* (New York: Harcourt, Brace and World, Inc., 1966), p. 157. Also *Jefferson Davis, Tragic Hero* (New York: Harcourt, Brace and World, Inc., 1964), p. 201.

"Reverently let us invoke the God of our fathers to guide and protect us in our efforts to perpetuate the principles which by His blessing they were able to vindicate, establish, and transmit to their posterity. With the continuance of His favor ever gratefully acknowledged, we may hopefully look forward to success, to peace, and to prosperity." The two Presidents differed radically in politics, but they were joined in reverence. To the delegation from the Christian forces of Chicago President Lincoln pointed out that "the rebel soldiers are praying with a great deal more earnestness, I fear, than our own troops, and expecting God to favor their side; for one of our soldiers, who had been taken prisoner, told Senator Wilson, a few days since, that he met with nothing so discouraging as the evident sincerity of those he was among in their prayers."[9]

A contemporary theologian, Karl A. Olsson, has noted that Lincoln's recognition of the sincerity of Southern piety was crucial for his own position. "He did not want," says Olsson, "to elevate his cause to the level of divine infallibility. He did not want the South to be damned and rejected as if it were only evil. And so, bowed down by the weight of his cares, he prayed. And the meekness of his prayer breathes in almost everything that he did."[10] In contrast to pronouncements which tend to be judgmental, prayer introduces men to a totally different dimension.

The fact that the prayers of the North and South obviously conflicted lent credence to a story in which President Lincoln took unusual delight. According to the common version of the story, two Quaker women, riding together on the train, began to compare the two Presidents.

"I think," said the first, "Jefferson will succeed."

"Why does thee think so?"

"Because Jefferson is a praying man."

9. *Collected Works*, V, p. 420.
10. Olsson, *Passion* (New York: Harper & Row, 1963), p. 28.

"And so is Abraham a praying man."

"Yes," came the punchline, "but the Lord will think Abraham is joking."

Of this, Lincoln said that it was the best story about himself that he had ever "read in the papers."[11] He loved it when piety and humor could be joined. That he could also combine courtesy and subtle humor is shown by the incident in which the King of Siam had offered President Buchanan, shortly before Lincoln's inauguration, a donation of elephants as breeding stock. On February 3, 1862, the straight-faced diplomat, taking care of Buchanan's correspondence, wrote:

I appreciate most highly Your Majesty's tender of good offices in forwarding to this Government a stock from which a supply of elephants might be raised on our own soil. This government would not hesitate to avail itself of so generous an offer if the object were one which could be made practically useful in the present condition of the United States.

Our political jurisdiction, however, does not reach a latitude so low as to favor the multiplication of the elephants, and steam on land, as well as on water, has been our best and most efficient agent of transportation in internal commerce.[12]

As we contemplate such a lightness of touch, we see the point of Professor Wolf's pertinent remark, "The picture then of Lincoln in the White House as the man of prayer needs the supplement of Lincoln as the man of laughter."[13]

The modern reader, cognizant of the multiplicity of demands upon Lincoln, may be surprised to learn that the Chief Executive found some time to deepen his spiritual life by reading from the devotional classics. We have evidence that he did so. Of all the

11. One version appeared in the Salem (Illinois) *Advertiser,* November 19, 1863, the same day as that of the Gettysburg Address.

12. *Collected Works,* V, p. 126.

13. *Lincoln's Religion,* p. 140.

interpreters of the inner life, few have equaled Richard Baxter (1615–1691). Baxter is famous both for his own *Autobiography* and his devotional guide, *Saint's Everlasting Rest*. Much that he wrote was produced during the turmoil of the English Civil War and some of it reached the mind of a thoughtful leader in the Civil War of America. The evidence that Lincoln read Baxter consists of an extract, written in his own hand.[14] The topic is the conflict between doubt and assurance, a conflict which we know was never totally resolved in Lincoln's mind. We must remember that Lincoln was never wholly free from melancholy, and this was something which the Puritan scholar understood very well. Baxter taught that, while doubt cannot be *expelled*, it can be *subdued*. This was Lincoln's experience exactly. The quoted passage, as printed by Barton, is: "It is more pleasing to God to see His people study Him and His will directly, than to spend the first and chief of their effort about attaining comfort for themselves. We have faith given us principally that we might believe and live by it in daily applications of Christ. You may believe immediately (by God's help) but getting assurance of it may be the work of a great part of your life."

By study of the quotation we obtain an important insight into Lincoln's theology. The copied words show that Lincoln was more concerned with the effort to know God's will than he was with the problem of his own personal salvation. Because he was not concerned primarily with the salvation of his own soul, his theology was marked by objectivity. He overcame his own melancholy, not by taking his own spiritual temperature, but by finding a work to do which made him forget himself.

The period of Lincoln's second election, though not as much a time of strain as the autumn two years before, was, neverthe-

14. See William E. Barton, *The Soul of Abraham Lincoln*, pp. 289, 290. Barton affirmed that he owned the half page of note paper, but he was in error in referring to the ownership by Winfield Smith, a one-time member of Lincoln's Cabinet. Barton may have meant to refer to Caleb Blood Smith, Lincoln's Secretary of the Interior, who died in December, 1862.

less, one which caused Lincoln to draw upon his deepest resources. The President fully believed for a while that he would
not be reelected. There was ample precedent for this expectation.
He became, in fact, the first President from one of the Northern
states to be twice elected. His opponent, General George McClellan, while carrying only three states, Kentucky, New Jersey, and
Delaware, received almost 45 percent of the popular vote. Lincoln was grateful for the confidence of those who supported him
so loyally in his difficult task, but he was deeply sobered by the
fact that almost two million of his fellow countrymen had voted
against him. An especially bitter blow was the loss of Sangamon
County, in which he had lived for many years.

When the election was over, the President responded with one
of his memorable affirmations of where his strength lay. "I
should," he said, "be the veriest shallow and self-conceited block-
head upon the footstool, if, in my discharge of the duties which
are put upon me in this place, I should hope to get along without
the wisdom which comes from God and not from men." Lincoln
said this to Noah Brooks on November 11, 1864. His reference
to the earth as the footstool is one of the many indications of the
influence of the Bible upon his speech. He knew this term well,
because its use in the Sermon on the Mount (Matthew 5:35) is
only one of several in the Scriptures.

The conversation with Brooks, together with the practice of
prayer, helps the student of Lincoln's thinking to understand
better his conception of God. It is admitted by all that he *grew*,
but in what direction did he grow? Nearly all the evidence shows
that he grew conspicuously in his recognition of God as personal.
At one time Lincoln was quoted, in a private conversation, as
saying that his conception of God was the same as that of nature,
and therefore impersonal.[15] It is conceivable that he once made
such a remark, but the weight of evidence is consistently at vari-

15. For this incident see Sandburg, *Abraham Lincoln, The War Years*, III, p. 381.

ance with this report. Increasingly, he felt that he was dealing, not with some impersonal Force able neither to know nor to care, but with One who guides tirelessly toward the fulfillment of His purpose. Only in this intellectual context does the idea of man as an instrument of God's will make sense.

We understand Lincoln's conception of God far better if we pay close attention, not to what he said in argument or in banter, but to the logical implications of his own practice, particularly the practice of prayer and his calls to prayer on the part of his fellow citizens. In prayer he combined the search for guidance with humble thanks. Both of these are meaningless unless the relationship to God can be a truly personal one, which, following Martin Buber, we now call an "I-Thou relationship." One cannot thank a Force; thanksgiving is unreasonable except in a personal connection.

Lincoln's own accounts of how he was led to turn to prayer as his greatest resource give us the clearest picture we have of his understanding of the Divine-human encounter. To the Baltimore Presbyterian Synod he confided more intimately than was his usual custom when he said, "I was early brought to a living reflection that nothing in my power whatever, in others to rely upon, would succeed without the direct assistance of the Almighty." It was in connection with these intimate remarks that the humble man said words which belong to the classic literature of witness, "I have often wished that I was a more devout man than I am." Following them came his account of his own major decision: "Nevertheless, amid the greatest difficulties of my Administration, when I could not see any other resort, I would place my whole reliance in God."[16]

Many have wondered why William H. Herndon, the Springfield lawyer who wrote voluminously about Lincoln after his

16. *Collected Works*, VI, pp. 535, 536.

assassination, could have referred to his former law partner as an unbeliever. The answer to this question lies partly in the character of Herndon, who overreacted to the claims of some that Lincoln was an orthodox Christian. But, more importantly, Herndon failed to understand because he did not really know Lincoln in the crucial years when the agony of decision drove him to spiritual depths which he had not formerly experienced. What we now know is that the four years of heavy responsibility, when the temptation to waver was never-ending, were also years of growth. Allan Nevins has reminded us that Lincoln's burden was made even more onerous because he had had no previous experience in administration.[17] It is really no wonder that he said God was his only hope.

One aspect of Lincoln's theology, which disturbed some of his Illinois neighbors, was his conviction that God would not in the end be defeated, even by man's sin and foolishness. Consequently, he said he could not believe that the omnipotent love of God is consistent with vindictiveness or "the endless punishment of any one of the human race." This he affirmed in his office in Springfield as late as 1859. But it would be a serious mistake to infer from such a remark that Lincoln denied the reasonableness of divine punishment. He saw punishment as parental in its object, "intended for the good of the offender," and more and more he applied this to the nation as well as to the individual person. Without this conception, much of the Second Inaugural is incomprehensible.

If Lincoln was a universalist in his conception of God's ultimate victory, he was not one to draw from this the practical conclusion of softness. Indeed, he said it would be better if preachers would talk less of pardon for sin and more of punishment. As Professor Wolf has observed, this was "the prophetic

17. *Lincoln and the Gettysburg Address,* edited by Allan Nevins (Urbana: University of Illinois Press, 1964), p. 4. (Hereafter called Nevins.)

note of a God of mercy Who punishes the sins of men in the judgments of history with a view to reformation."[18] In short, following what he considered to be the essential teaching of Christ, and accepting what he called "the provisions of the gospel system," Lincoln was able to include, in the magnitude of his thought, both sternness and hope. Certainly he did not fall into the heresy described by Archbishop William Temple, which involves "a conception of God as so genially tolerant as to be morally indifferent."[19] Lincoln understood God, whom he faced directly in personal encounter, not as One who is morally indifferent, but as the Infinite Person who gives meaning to the moral order. This provided the note of sternness from which Lincoln never wavered, even though he also believed in God's ultimate triumph. It is this theological context which gives meaning to Lincoln's best-known quotation from Thomas Jefferson, "I tremble for my country when I remember that God is just!" There was a wide difference in theology between Jefferson and Lincoln, but on this point they were agreed.[20] Because both men accepted the idea of "God's eternal justice," they did not hesitate to speak of God's "wrath." More and more, as Lincoln engaged in both prayer and thought, he became convinced that the Civil War had to be understood in such terms.

During his forty-nine months in the presidency Abraham Lincoln issued nine separate calls to public penitence, fasting, prayer, and thanksgiving. These calls have not received the attention which they deserve. Seen together they reveal with remarkable clarity both the growth and the depth of the man's inner life. Study of these documents is, indeed, a self-justifying undertaking. They are important in what they reveal, not only about

18. *Lincoln's Religion*, p. 105.

19. *Nature, Man and God* (London: Macmillan and Co., Ltd., 1934), p. 456.

20. The reference to Jefferson came in a long address at Columbus, Ohio, on September 16, 1859. See *Collected Works*, III, p. 410.

Abraham Lincoln, but also about the total American experiment. Though these are relatively unknown, they demonstrate almost as well as the famous speeches the grandeur of Lincoln's mature style, both in thought and in expression. He was breaking new ground and he was aware that he was doing so.

Lincoln produced his first public call to prayer on August 12, 1861, the day assigned being the last Thursday in September. The pattern, thus established in Lincoln's first year as President, of calling for a special observance on *Thursday*, was continued with only two exceptions. One advantage of choosing Thursday was that this day in the middle of the week was not identified with any existing worshiping group. Thus it could belong equally to all of the people, regardless of denominational affiliations. The people were called, not as churchmen, but as Americans! The distribution of the special proclamations was as follows; 1861, two; 1862, one; 1863, three; 1864, three. Just before his death, as his last public address tells us, Lincoln was contemplating a tenth such Proclamation. Only three days before he was shot, the President made his reverent purpose known to the people. "The evacuation of Petersburg and Richmond," he said, "and the surrender of the principal insurgent army, give hope of a righteous and speedy peace whose joyous expression can not be restrained. In the midst of this, however, He, from Whom all blessings flow, must not be forgotten. A call for a national thanksgiving is being prepared, and will be duly promulgated."[21]

The first of the nine calls to prayer was suggested and even requested by a joint committee of both Houses of Congress. Recommended was "a day of public humiliation, prayer and fasting to be observed by the people of the United States." This first Proclamation had no hint of rejoicing, for there was, in fact, nothing about which the people could reasonably rejoice. What

21. *Collected Works*, VIII, pp. 399, 400.

was required, Lincoln concluded, was not boasting but humility. In his eloquent development of this theme we sense one of the first intimations of the new Lincoln style which was to emerge from the fire of disappointment.

Lincoln's own part in the memorable pronouncement[22] began with the recognition that "it is fit and becoming in all people, at all times, to acknowledge and revere the Supreme Government of God; to bow in humble submission to his chastisements; to confess and deplore their sins and transgressions in the full conviction that the fear of the Lord is the beginning of wisdom; and to pray, with all fervency and contrition, for the pardon of their past offences, and for a blessing upon their present and prospective action." Here is no suggestion of vindictiveness toward the people of the Confederacy and not one judgmental line. In this first "National Fast Day," the emphasis was upon personal contrition rather than upon blame of others.

This remarkable literary production provides us with a direct insight into Lincoln's own theology of anguish, in which he saw all Americans involved. He understood the war, not as an accident of history, but as a "terrible visitation" revealing "the hand of God." In the following paragraph, Abraham Lincoln was revealing both to his contemporaries and to future generations his own deepest conviction about God and man.

And whereas when our own beloved Country, once, by blessing of God, united, prosperous, and happy, is now afflicted with factions and civil war, it is peculiarly fit for us to recognize the hand of God in this terrible visitation, and in sorrowful remembrance of our own faults and crimes as a nation and as individuals, to humble ourselves before Him, and to pray for His mercy,—to pray that we may be spared further punishment, though most justly deserved; that our arms may be blessed and made effectual for the re-establishment of law, order and peace, throughout the wide extent of our country; and that the inestimable

22. *Collected Works*, IV, p. 482.

boon of civil and religious liberty, earned under His guidance and blessing, by the labors and sufferings of our fathers, may be restored in all
its original excellence.

Here, in the authentic form, is the Lincoln style of the final
chapter of his life. By this time, whatever personal pride he had
ever had was thoroughly chastened and he could refer to prayer
in a completely unapologetic fashion. The entire purpose of the
effort was "to the end that the united prayer of the nation may
ascend to the Throne of Grace and bring down plentiful blessings upon our Country." Prayer, in the President's mind, had by
August 12, 1861, become an experience of genuine magnitude. It
included both petitions and praise; it began with repentance, but
it did not end there; it was as meaningful for a whole people as
for a solitary individual.

No really important call was made in the bleak year of 1862,
but by March 30, 1863, the new Lincoln showed himself with
both moral and literary grandeur. Again, as in 1861, the President called for a "National Fast Day." The day assigned was
Thursday, April 30. This occasion was initiated by the United
States Senate, which in a resolution requested the President to set
apart a day for "National prayer and humiliation." It is important to remember that the Emancipation Proclamation had been
put into effect three months prior to the new proclamation, and
that the turning point of the Battle of Gettysburg was still three
months in the future. The outcome at this time was therefore far
from certain. But in spite of uncertainty about the outcome, there
was no uncertainty about the conviction. Accordingly, here, in
the spring of 1863, two years prior to his death, we find the
grandeur of Lincoln's written style which subsequent generations have learned to associate with his name. "And whereas," he
said, "it is the duty of nations as well as of men, to own their
dependence upon the overruling power of God, to confess their

sins and transgressions, in humble sorrow, yet with assured hope that genuine repentance will lead to mercy and pardon; and to recognize the sublime truth, announced in the Holy Scriptures and proven by all history, that those nations only are blessed whose God is the Lord."

What were the national sins of which the Chief Magistrate was painfully conscious? They were the sins of pride, arising from the conviction of self-sufficiency. "Intoxicated with unbroken success, we have become too self-sufficient to feel the necessity of redeeming and preserving grace, too proud to pray to the God that made us!" The prayer requested was the double one, "the pardon of our national sins, and the restoration of our now divided and suffering Country." Terrible as it was, the ordeal might, Lincoln believed, turn into a blessing if it could induce true humility. With this high hope in mind, the call was made as follows:

Now, therefore, in compliance with the request, and fully concurring in the views of the Senate, I do, by this proclamation, designate and set apart Thursday, the 30th day of April, 1863, as a day of national humiliation, fasting and prayer. And I do hereby request all the people to abstain, on that day, from their ordinary secular pursuits, and to unite, at their several places of public worship and their respective homes, in keeping the day holy to the Lord, and devoted to the humble discharge of the religious duties proper to that solemn occasion.[23]

After Gettysburg, President Lincoln's expressions, in his Proclamations, were a little less somber in that he referred not only to "sorrow," but also to "triumph." The call for Thursday, August 6, 1863, was not for a Fast Day, but for a day devoted to "Thanksgiving, Praise and Prayer." Another innovation, after Gettysburg, was a reference to the "insurgents." What he asked for, however, was not judgment upon them, but prayer for a change in their hearts. He asked the citizens to pray, specifically,

23. *Collected Works*, VI, p. 156.

for God "to subdue the anger, which has produced, and so long sustained a needless and cruel rebellion, to change the hearts of the insurgents, to guide the counsels of the Government with wisdom adequate to so great a national emergency, and to visit with tender care and consolation throughout the length and breadth of our land all those who, through the vicissitudes of marches, voyages, battles and sieges, have been brought to suffer in mind, body or estate, and finally to lead the whole nation, through the paths of repentance and submission to the Divine Will, back to the perfect enjoyment of Union and fraternal peace."[24]

The style of these three Proclamations is very impressive. It is vastly superior to that of the First Inaugural, indicating remarkable growth in only a few months. In the calls to prayer Lincoln became independent of Seward's tutelage, as he was not when the First Inaugural was composed. Today, as we read William Seward's own writings, we are aware, of course, that we are in contact with a fine clear mind, but his literary sense was slight in comparison with that of the mature and independent Lincoln. Many have noted Lincoln's capacity for growth, but no one expressed it better than did his one-time critic, Horace Greeley, editor of the New York *Tribune*. "Never before," he said, "did one so constantly and visibly *grow* under the discipline of incessant cares, anxieties and trials. The Lincoln of '62 was plainly a larger, broader, better man than he had been in '61; while '63 and '64 worked his continued and unabated growth in mental and moral stature."[25]

While Lincoln's growth was evident in many phases of his life, it was especially so in the development of his religious thinking.

24. Ibid., p. 332.
25. Greeley's address on Lincoln was published nearly twenty years after his own death in *The Century Illustrated Monthly Magazine*, XLII, pp. 371–382. The statement printed here appears on p. 381.

The magnificence of the Fast Day Proclamations arises from this kind of growth as much as it stems from the increased capacity for nobility of expression. He was able to write nobly about prayer, because prayer had come to dominate his thinking. The idea that there could be direct communication between finite minds and the Infinite Mind had become, for Lincoln, an idea of overwhelming magnitude.

The special call to thanksgiving, as well as to prayer, which came after the victory at Gettysburg, provided an introduction for the first annual Thanksgiving observed later in 1863. Thanksgiving Day, as we know it now, was never known prior to Lincoln's decision. There had, of course, been sporadic celebrations, dating back to the early plantations in both Virginia and Massachusetts, but these were in no sense national or regularized. Though some of the states had made experiments along this line, the celebrations achieved only local significance. Lincoln, himself, made a local beginning on the last Thursday of November, 1861, but the announcement came only one day in advance, and those addressed included only the residents of Washington and Georgetown.[26] In his first year of office this was all that occurred to the harassed President, so far as a November observance was concerned. In November, 1862, which was still a time of severe strain, nothing was done in this connection. In 1863, however, all was different. In that momentous year, the year of the Gettysburg Address, the President inaugurated a practice of far-reaching significance, which has been continued by all of his successors to the present day.

The credit for the modern conception of Thanksgiving as an established National Festival belongs primarily to an otherwise obscure woman, Sara Josepha Hale. On September 28, 1863, Miss Hale, "Editress of the *Lady's Book*," wrote to the President re-

26. For the brief announcement see *Collected Works*, V, p. 32.

questing a few minutes of his time in order to lay before him "a subject of deep interest." Her proposal was simply that the scattered celebrations of Thanksgiving be unified into "a National and fixed Union Festival." Since the idea appealed to Lincoln, there was issued on October 3, 1863, the first of many such Proclamations. In the rush of duties Lincoln assigned to Seward some of the task of writing this document, with the result that it is not equal, in literary appeal, to the two Fast Day Proclamations.

The first National Thanksgiving Proclamation includes the now familiar Lincoln themes of the sternness of the moral law and of God's mercy. Our eyes are directed to "the Most High God, who, while dealing with us in anger for our sins, hath nevertheless remembered mercy." What is expressed is an almost perfect balance between gratitude, penitence, and compassion. The people are called, says the Proclamation, not only to give thanks for "singular deliverances and blessings," but also to "humble penitence for our national perverseness and disobedience." The people, finally, are asked to "commend to His tender care all those who have become widows, orphans, mourners or sufferers in the lamentable civil strife in which we are unavoidably engaged, and fervently implore the interposition of the Almighty Hand to heal the wounds of the nation and to restore it as soon as may be consistent with the Divine purposes to the full enjoyment of peace, harmony, tranquillity and Union."[27]

The first Thanksgiving Proclamation is revealing in what it does not say. No longer are people asked to assemble in their customary places of worship. The citizens are not called to prayer as Protestants or Jews or Roman Catholics, but as members of a common family. Where they gather is not important! Any secular building would be entirely suitable for this high purpose. Though the new conception is unashamedly religious,

27. *Collected Works*, VI, p. 497.

it is in no sense ecclesiastical. Lincoln was taking seriously the idea which had grown upon him for a long time, that God is able to call a *nation*. God, he believed, calls a nation to service, especially that of liberation from bondage of all kinds, but He also calls the nation to prayer. It was Lincoln's mature conclusion that, if the people are not obedient to the latter, they will not long be obedient to the former. After years of mental struggle, Abraham Lincoln was at last performing a prophetic role. With characteristic honesty, he did not ask the people to engage in practices in which he did not, himself, engage.

It seemed that the war would never end. After the jubilation of part of 1863, and the elevated emotion at the Gettysburg Battlefield in November, there was a general sense of despair. Thousands of good men, the same kind of men, were killed on both sides, and the end seemed always to be unattainable. Accordingly, both Houses of Congress joined in a resolution on July 2, 1864, asking for yet another day of "humiliation and prayer by the people of the United States." Lincoln willingly concurred, and the authentic Lincoln style appeared again. This time, with absolute simplicity, he called the day a "Day of Prayer." The date assigned was the first Thursday in August.

The Proclamation dated July 7, 1864, carries further the brooding thoughts of the Fast Day Proclamations, revealing with accuracy the inner life of the man in the White House. Like others, Lincoln had had to face the possibility of failure of his grandest hopes. Perhaps the American Union would be permanently fractured and the continent Balkanized. Perhaps, after eighty-eight years, the dream could fade. In the light of such realism Lincoln asked his fellow citizens to pray earnestly to Almighty God and "to implore Him, as the Supreme Ruler of the World, not to destroy us as a people, nor suffer us to be destroyed by the hostility or connivance of other Nations, or by obstinate adhesion to our own counsels, which may be in conflict with His eternal purposes, and to implore Him to enlighten the mind of the Nation to know and do His will; humbly believing that it is in accordance with His will that our place should be maintained as a united people among the family of nations."[28] If any person sincerely desires to know what Abraham Lincoln really believed, the Proclamation which he made one year after the Battle of Gettysburg will provide the answer. Never, until the very end, was the conviction of a holy calling for an entire people more brilliantly expressed.

The last of Lincoln's nine calls to prayer was written October 20, 1864, again setting apart the last Thursday of November as a time of National Thanksgiving. Miss Hale had, on October 9, written to Secretary Seward, encouraging a repetition of the action of a year before and enclosing proof of her article on the subject which was due to appear in the November issue of the *Lady's Book*. "I send," she wrote, "a copy of the proof for the President. You will greatly oblige me by handing this to him and acquainting him with the contents of this letter. I do not like to trouble him with a note. Should the president see fit to issue his proclamation at once, the important paper would reach the knowledge of American citizens in Europe and Asia, as well as throughout our wide land."

The President responded at once, dating his last Proclamation of this character October 20, 1864. The Proclamation, which was relatively brief, was remarkable chiefly for its opening sentence, which was an unadorned statement of the fact that total disaster, feared by so many, had not occurred. "It has pleased Almighty God," the Proclamation began, "to prolong our national life another year." The document reflects no easy optimism, but neither does it reflect despair. "He has been pleased," wrote Lincoln, "to animate and inspire our minds and hearts with fortitude, courage

28. *Collected Works*, VII, p. 431.

and resolution sufficient for the great trial of civil war into which we have been brought by our own adherence as a nation to the cause of Freedom and Humanity, and to afford to us reasonable hopes of an ultimate and happy deliverance from all our dangers and afflictions."[29]

Valuable as the public Proclamations are, they represent only one of many sources for our knowledge of the depths of Abraham Lincoln's religious experience. What is increasingly obvious is that he attempted to express a faith for the entire people, regardless of denominational affiliation. His appeal was directed to Jews as well as to Christians. He did not hesitate, on some occasions, to refer to Christ as the "Savior." But as President of the whole people he sought to point primarily to the One whom Christ revealed, and who, he believed, is the Father of all.

Abraham Lincoln was not a religious leader in the conventional sense. Certainly he was not professionally religious and he had no formal theological training. What he knew about prayer came not from books, but from experience, much of it agonizing. He was no flaming prophet like John the Baptist, nor was he an ecstatic arouser of men's emotions, like the Mahdi. He was, instead, as Horace Greeley said, "a plain, true, earnest patriotic man, gifted with common sense." What lifted him above others of this type was the overwhelming conviction that God's will could be partly known and that the only hope for finite men lay in conformity to that will. His deepest conviction about prayer was that which he expressed on March 30, 1863, when he appealed to his fellow citizens to "rest humbly in the hope authorized by the Divine teachings that the united cry of the Nation will be heard on high, and answered with blessings."[30]

29. *Collected Works*, VIII, p. 55.
30. *Collected Works*, VI, p. 156.

5
Lincoln and the Church

Blessed be God, Who, in this our great trial, giveth us the churches.

ABRAHAM LINCOLN

Did Lincoln's theology require that he be a member of a particular church? The short answer is that it did not; but, because the subject is a more complicated one than it at first appears to be, the short answer does not suffice. The subject of church membership is one which is often introduced whenever Lincoln's religion is discussed. That he never became a church member is the one phase of this subject which numerous people know. What is strange is that the failure to join a church is often interpreted as evidence that the Civil War President had no strong or vital faith. It is important to show why this popular conclusion is unjustified.

Lincoln's failure to become a church member is better understood when we realize how people generally felt about membership in his own lifetime. In our generation it is normally expected that a serious Christian will automatically join a particular congregation, but this was not so in Lincoln's day. The modern American is surprised to learn that only 23 percent of the population were church members in 1860, the year in which Lincoln won his first election to the Presidency. A hundred years later more than 60 percent were church members. In short, the President's lack of membership was something which he shared with the great majority of his fellow citizens. When we know this we begin to see that the issue has been inflated out of proportion to its true significance.

In the light of our own presuppositions, it would seem natural for Lincoln to have joined the Pigeon Creek Church as a boy, particularly when he served as sexton for the meeting house. We get new perspective, however, when we learn that in the pioneer churches few young people were accepted into membership. Parents who were church members, says Dr. Louis A. Warren, tended to assume the responsibility for the spiritual guidance of their families. On the whole, people were not expected to apply for membership apart from the contemplation of matrimony, which, of course, was no part of Abraham Lincoln's experience at that time. His sister Sally followed the general practice by being received into membership on April 8, 1826, but if Abraham had also applied that would have seemed strange. It was because membership was taken seriously that it was normally reserved for maturity.[1] This is one of the reasons why church membership was comparatively small in all of early America.[2]

Since, for Americans of a century and more ago, the idea of the Church was not so central as it is in the latter half of the twentieth century, Abraham Lincoln was following the expected pattern of thought when his religion was centered far more in the Bible than in the Church. We tend to forget how recent the emphasis upon the significance of the fellowship of a gathered

1. See Warren, *Lincoln's Youth, Seven to Twenty-one*, pp. 151, 213.
2. See Franklin H. Littell, *From State Church to Pluralism* (New York: Doubleday and Company, 1962).

society really is. In most American theological circles this emphasis is not much more than sixty years in duration. One of the first influential treatments of the subject appeared in 1912 from the pen of T. R. Glover with the then fresh title, *The Nature and Purpose of a Christian Society.*

We are familiar now with the idea that it is impossible to be a Christian alone, and that it is only in the gathered fellowship that Christ is truly known. But in Lincoln's day very few authors were saying anything like this. It is doubtful, in fact, if Lincoln ever heard such teaching at all. Instead, we know that he heard much discussion of creedal statements, sometimes in a manner calculated to alienate him from whatever fellowship might have been available to him. With his excellent mind, he reacted negatively to some of the preaching which he heard, with the natural consequence that his major field of religious service soon came to be the civil rather than the ecclesiastical order. He felt at home in the Illinois legislature as he never did in any Illinois church. Indeed, he reported that he hesitated to attend church in Springfield for fear that he would not know how to act.[3]

Part of Lincoln's reluctance to identify entirely with a Christian body, especially in his pre-Washington experience, was his keen sense of intellectual honesty. He was determined not to act a part in which he could not be involved with absolute integrity. Furthermore, in his Illinois days Lincoln had good reason to feel wounded by unfair opposition on the part of church members, including some prominent clergymen. When, in 1846, Lincoln was elected to Congress as the Whig representative of the Seventh District of Illinois, his Democratic opponent was the old-fashioned Methodist circuit rider, Peter Cartwright. It is to Cartwright's discredit that he sought to make political capital out of the fact that Lincoln was not a church member. Lincoln had

3. His misgiving in this point is revealed in a letter addressed to Mary S. Owens, written May 7, 1837. *Collected Works,* I, p. 78.

faced this problem before, especially in 1843, when he reported of himself that there was the strangest combination of church influence against him. It was contended, he said, "that no Christian ought to go for me, because I belonged to no church."[4]

In our effort to judge the intensity of the conflict between the preacher and the young politician it is not necessary to rely on the folklore which developed and which some biographers have credited. We have Lincoln's own account of the controversy in a letter dated August 11, 1846, addressed to Allen N. Ford, who was editor of the *Gazette*, published at Lacon, Illinois. "Shortly before starting on my tour through yours, and the other Northern counties of the district," Lincoln wrote, "I was informed by letter from Jacksonville that Mr. Cartwright was whispering the charge of infidelity against me in that quarter. . . . I incline to the belief that he has succeeded in deceiving some honest men." Lincoln continued with a discussion of moral philosophy in which the key sentence is, "I believe it is an established maxim in morals that he who makes an assertion without knowing whether it is true or false, is guilty of falsehood."[5] Lincoln was too astute to condemn a denomination because of the act of one leader, but the lack of ethical sensitivity deeply shocked him. It seemed reasonable to him to expect that a sincere Christian would feel constrained to exhibit great care in guarding the reputations of others. The handbill printed in chapter one was produced as Lincoln's effort to counter what seemed to him to be an unfair attack, but he wisely refrained in the handbill from mentioning Cartwright by name.

This encounter with the circuit rider is highly revealing. At the age of thirty-seven Lincoln was not only somewhat anticlerical, but also reverent. He did not allow the ineptitude of the man

4. Letter to Martin S. Morris, dated March 26, 1843. *Collected Works*, I, pp. 319–321.

5. *Collected Works*, I, pp. 383, 384.

who claimed to represent the Gospel turn him against it. Lincoln was looking for morality in religion and resenting its absence. His campaign ended with success, but the mark on his inner life which the encounter left was a permanent one. He was now, at thirty-seven, a truly public man, as the only Whig Congressman elected from the State of Illinois, and he was beginning to achieve maturity in his inner life. It is most remarkable that Lincoln, when he saw so much that was vulnerable in the leadership of the Church, did not move to the opposite error and become a scoffer.

One insight into Lincoln's reticence we owe to Mrs. Rankin, a close friend of both contestants. Our source in this connection, already mentioned above, is Henry B. Rankin, Mrs. Rankin's son. Henry Rankin was at one time employed in Lincoln's law office and in 1916 he published his recollections. Since his published account deals with conversations which occurred seventy years earlier, and which he knew only from what his mother told him, we dare not accept its details uncritically. But the main point seems highly credible, partly because it is coherent with other known elements in Lincoln's character. One evening this friendly woman, from whom Lincoln had borrowed books, told him that, while she knew the Cartwright charges were false, she was still puzzled about Lincoln's true position. The question made Lincoln restless. He rose from his chair, rested an elbow on the mantel of the fireplace, and began to say slowly, "I will not discuss the character and religion of Jesus Christ on the stump! That is no place for it, though my opponent, a minister of His Gospel, thinks it is."[6]

Lincoln did not seek church membership as he entered spiritual maturity partly because he took his faith so seriously that he approached it with extreme reverence and consequent restraint. "Those days of trouble," he told Mrs. Rankin, "found

6. *Personal Recollections of Abraham Lincoln*, p. 323.

me tossed amid a sea of questionings. They piled big around me. Through all I groped my way until I found a stronger and higher grasp of thought, one that reached beyond this life with a clearness and satisfaction I had never known before. The Scriptures unfolded before me with a deeper and more logical appeal, through these new experiences than anything else I could find to turn to, or even before had found in them. I do not claim that all my doubts were removed then, or since that time have been swept away. They were not."

The opposition of the religious leaders to a man of Lincoln's originality continued up to the time of his first election to the presidency. In 1860, of the twenty-three pastors in the City of Springfield, only three appeared to be ready to vote for their fellow townsman. The record of the churches on slavery, in 1858, was something which deterred Lincoln's wholehearted allegiance to their work. Referring to slavery, in his last debate with Senator Douglas, Lincoln asked, "Does it not enter into the churches and rend them asunder? What divided the great Methodist Church into two parts, North and South? What has raised this constant disturbance in every Presbyterian General Assembly that meets? What disturbed the Unitarian Church in this very city two years ago?"[7] Lincoln was impatient with Christian organizations which could not unite in opposition to something as obvious as the sinfulness of human slavery. A man of less pronounced integrity might simply have joined the Episcopal or the Presbyterian Church, thereby stopping the mouths of some of his critics. Since Lincoln refused to do this, he was left in a difficult position politically. He was too perplexed to please the conventional and too reverent to please the infidels.

Lincoln came close to membership when his wife joined the First Presbyterian Church of Springfield in 1852. At that time he

7. This debate was held at Alton on October 15, 1858. *Collected Works*, III, p. 310.

rented a pew, for which he paid fifty dollars annually, and which he occupied when he was in the city. It is significant that Lincoln attended, not only the regular meetings for worship, but the inquiry meetings also. After becoming President, his relationship to the New York Avenue Presbyterian Church, in Washington, was similar to the one experienced in Springfield. As before, he paid fifty dollars a year in pew rental, occupying the pew which had formerly been assigned to President Buchanan. He soon came to regard Dr. Phineas D. Gurley of the New York Avenue Church as his pastor, receiving him frequently in the White House. It has been reported that Lincoln had made arrangements to become a member officially on Easter Day, and that, apart from his assassination, he would have taken this step. Though this is possible, we have no way of verifying the truth of the report. The chief evidence against it is that Dr. Gurley, so far as we know, never mentioned it publicly. The determination to join, if accurate, would have been extremely newsworthy. It would have been reasonable for Dr. Gurley to have mentioned it at the funeral in the White House, in which he delivered the sermon which has been preserved. The only evidence we have is an affidavit signed more than sixty years later by Mrs. Sidney I. Lauck, then a very old woman. In her affidavit signed under oath in Essex County, New Jersey, February 15, 1928, she said, "After Mr. Lincoln's death, Dr. Gurley told me that Mr. Lincoln had made all the necessary arrangements with him and the Session of the New York Avenue Presbyterian Church to be received into the membership of the said church, by confession of his faith in Christ, on the Easter Sunday following the Friday night when Mr. Lincoln was assassinated." Mrs. Lauck was, she said, about thirty years of age at the time of the assassination.[8]

Possibly no subject has developed more folklore than that of

8. See Frank E. Edgington, *A History of the New York Avenue Presbyterian Church* (Washington, D. C., 1961), pp. 244, 245.

Lincoln's church affiliation. The claims which have been made are so numerous that it would be difficult to mention all of them. It has been asserted that Lincoln was baptized as a Campbellite, that he was a Swedenborgian, that he was a Spiritualist, etc., but not one such claim has been verified. Lincoln was sufficiently ecumenical in spirit to have connections with a great many different movements, but he was never much of a joiner. When asked directly whether he was a Mason, Lincoln expressed his admiration for the order, but went on to say that he had never joined it.

It has sometimes been supposed that Lincoln's failure to join a particular church was based upon his rejection of all denominationalism. But there is abundant evidence to show that this is not the case. We are far closer to the truth when we say that his admiration for many different denominations increased his problem in fastening upon any one to the exclusion of all of the others. Far from denigrating the rise of denominations, he expressed gratitude for the existence of each of several.

On one occasion one of Lincoln's friends lamented in his presence the divided condition of Protestantism and the consequent number of individual churches, only to find that Lincoln rejected the popular cliché. The essence of the response was that the man was wasting his tears. "My good brother," he said, "you are all wrong. The more sects we have the better. They are all getting somebody in that the others could not: and even with the numerous divisions we are all doing tolerably well."[9] Essential to Lincoln's mature theology was what we may truly call a sophisticated ecumenicity. He did not think the proliferation of denominations was evil, provided each was sufficiently humble to learn from the others and also providing each preserved something of value which, apart from its corporate existence, might

9. *The Making of a Minister: The Autobiography of Clarence E. McCartney,* edited by J. Clyde Henry (Great Neck, N. Y.: Channel Press, 1961).

be lost. That he felt this about Quakerism was increasingly obvious, though he never seriously considered becoming a Quaker, as some of his ancestors were. Lincoln in his maturity outgrew any hostility he once felt toward the Methodism of Peter Cartwright. This is indicated by his generous and well-known words, "God bless the Methodist Church."

Lincoln sought to be even-handed in his treatment of Roman Catholics, as with the various Protestant denominations. Though he had no precedent for appointing chaplains to hospitals, Lincoln recognized the need and acted on his own responsibility. On October 21, 1861, he wrote to Archbishop John J. Hughes offering to appoint Catholic chaplains on the same basis as Protestants.[10] Priests were assigned duties October 24, 1861.

The President's responses to the various denominational delegations became the occasions for some of his most quotable declarations. A splendid example of this occurred, as Lincoln's new firmness was beginning to assume shape, when on May 13, 1862, he received a Lutheran delegation of national scope. "I welcome here," he said, "the representatives of the Evangelical Lutherans of the United States. I accept with gratitude their assurances of the sympathy and support of that enlightened, influential, and loyal class of my fellow citizens in an important crisis which involves, in my judgment, not only the civil and religious liberties of our own dear land, but in a large degree the civil and religious liberties of mankind in many countries and through many ages." It was people of this character who could bring out the noblest strain in the President's emergent thinking. "You may all recollect," he concluded, "that in taking up the sword thus forced into our hands this government appealed to the prayers of the pious and the good, and declared that it placed its whole dependence upon the favor of God. I now humbly and rever-

10. *Collected Works*, IV, p. 559.

ently, in your presence, reiterate the acknowledgment of that dependence, not doubting that, if it shall please the Divine Being who determines the destinies of nations that this shall remain a united people, they will, humbly seeking the Divine guidance, make their prolonged national existence a source of new benefits to themselves and their successors, and to all classes and conditions of mankind."[11]

One important factor in Lincoln's new appreciation for the churches was the growing contrast between their response to his efforts and the reactions of other sectors of the population, especially the press. At the same time that the members of the churches seemed to understand his predicament better, many of the editors understood it less. Some of the most cruel of all of the editorial criticism came in 1864, prior to his renomination and reelection. For example, the New York *Herald,* prior to the Baltimore Convention, referred to the President as "joke incarnated, his election a very sorry joke, and the idea that such a man as he should be the President of such a country as this, a very ridiculous joke." Even more strident was the New Year's, 1864, edition of the *Crisis:*

The people of the North owe Mr. Lincoln nothing but eternal hatred and scorn. There are 500,000 new made graves; there are 500,000 orphans; there are 200,000 widows; there is a bottomless sea of blood; there is the Constitution broken; there are liberty and law—liberty in chains and in a dungeon; thieves in the Treasury, provost marshals in the seats of justice, butchers in the pulpit—and these are the things which we owe Mr. Lincoln.

In reaction to such vituperation, Lincoln turned more and more to the Church rather than to the press. In the Church he found people who, though they hated war as much as the editors hated it, saw with clarity what the moral alternative was. Conse-

11. *Collected Works,* V, pp. 212, 213.

quently, the beleaguered President went out of his way to be generous with church requests. This explains one of Mrs. Gurney's letters in which she wrote, "I think I may venture to say that Friends are not less loyal for the leniency with which their honest convictions have been treated, and I believe there are very few amongst us who would not lament to see any other than Abraham Lincoln fill the Presidential chair, at least at the next election."

Respecting all denominations as he did, President Lincoln was resolute in refusing to give special privileges to any or to interfere in ecclesiastical decisions. A difficult situation developed in St. Louis when the Reverend Samuel B. McPheeters was expelled from the pastorate of the Pine Street Presbyterian Church because of what the majority of the members considered "unmistakable evidence of sympathy with the rebellion." When President Lincoln was handed a harsh petition from the ousted pastor's supporters, he replied with a strong affirmation of his own policy of noninterference and the refusal to give privileges to a clergyman which would not be given to anyone else. "I directed, a long time ago," he said, "that Dr. McPheters was to be arrested, or remain at large, upon the same rule as any one else."[12] Lincoln was even more explicit in a letter written February 11, 1864, to Edwin M. Stanton, the Secretary of War. "When an individual, in the church or out of it, becomes dangerous to the public interest, he must be checked; but the churches, as such, must take care of themselves."[13]

Lincoln's final attitude, then, toward the churches was respect for all, combined with refusal to interfere with any. His simple remark to Mrs. Gurney, "I am much indebted to the good Christian people of the country," went to the heart of the matter.

12. *Collected Works*, VII, p. 86. Lincoln spelled the controversial pastor's name "McPheters."
13. Ibid., pp. 86, 178, 179.

Indeed, Lincoln's new attitude toward the churches is one of the chief marks of the radical change in his spiritual life which occurred during the years of supreme crisis. To Lincoln's amazement he found that the Church, which had seemed to him for years to be perhaps worth while, but not very important, had become his strongest organized support. We have to reach into the twentieth century, with its fierce turmoil in the persecution of the German Jews, to find an adequate parallel. Those who know it will not soon forget Albert Einstein's appreciation of the Church as a strong moral ally, and his consequent laconic remark, "I am forced to confess that what I once despised I now praise unreservedly." The question of Lincoln's church membership is, in spite of the attention which it has received, relatively trivial, but his new admiration of the Church and its potent moral witness is not trivial at all.

Lincoln's matured conception of Church and State was not one of absolute separation. Complete separation would have forbidden the establishment of a Federal celebration of Thanksgiving, a point which some contemporary protesters are quick to see. We realize how far removed Lincoln was from a total separation between religion and the government when we note that no other President has called the nation to prayer, fasting, and thanksgiving as often as Lincoln did. That he was not trying to bypass the organized churches is shown by the fact that both of the remarkable Fast Day Proclamations recognize the importance of the organized worshiping groups. In calling the first Fast Day in September, 1861, the support of the religious leaders was specifically solicited. The President recommended to all the people, and especially to all ministers and teachers of religion of all denominations, that they should gather on the day in question "according to their several creeds and modes of worship."[14] Thereby, ecumenicity was encouraged by the chief theologian of

14. *Collected Works*, IV, p. 482.

civil religion. The spiritual needs of the agonized state were not met by denying the values of the various denominations and congregations, but rather by exalting them.

Lincoln grew markedly in his respect for the Church as an institution, but that did not mean that he was on good terms with all church people or with all of the clergy. Indeed, the late Reinhold Niebuhr concluded that many of the religious leaders of the period, in spite of their good will, were inferior to Lincoln theologically. Consequently, Niebuhr began his brilliant chapter "The Religion of Abraham Lincoln" by saying: "Analysis of the religion of Abraham Lincoln in the context of the traditional religion of his time and place and of its polemical use on the slavery issue, which corrupted religious life in the days before and during the Civil War, must lead to the conclusion that Lincoln's religious convictions were superior in depth and purity to those, not only of the political leaders of his day, but of the religious leaders of the era."[15]

The President found it hard to be patient with some clergymen, especially with those who were perfectly certain that they knew exactly how the nation should proceed. Prime examples of such certitude were provided by both the clergy who belonged to the peace party and those who were extreme Abolitionists. "I am approached," said Lincoln, "with the most opposite opinions and advice, and that by religious men, who are equally certain that they represent the Divine will."[16] The Chaplain of the Senate, the Reverend Byron Sunderland, clearly irked the President by his tendency to turn his prayers into lectures, informing the Almighty on subjects of all kinds. In one prayer, for instance, he alluded critically to Lincoln's having been at the theater the night before. The Chaplain's performance led Senator Willard Saulsbury of Delaware to offer a resolution requesting the Chaplain "to pray to and supplicate Almighty God in our behalf, and not

15. Nevins, p. 72.
16. *Collected Works*, V, pp. 419, 420.

to lecture Him." When the President was trying with all his might to bring the war to an end, he did not appreciate the cruel attacks of a few preachers who supposed they understood the situation better than he did. Even the famous Henry Ward Beecher said, in reference to Lincoln, "Not a spark of genius has he; not an element of leadership. Not one particle of heroic enthusiasm."[17] We know now, of course, that this cruelly judgmental stance hurt Beecher more in the long run than it hurt the man against whom it was directed, but at the time it was not easy to bear.

In regard to slavery and emancipation President Lincoln felt and appreciated most keenly the support of church bodies. In all of the church conventions which met soon after the preliminary proclamation of emancipation announced on September 22, 1862, the President's crucial decision was greeted with the heartiest expressions of approval and support. This was doubly appreciated by the man at the helm because there were others who ridiculed his move. John Nicolay and John Hay saw that the growing affinity between Lincoln and church groups was produced by the common struggle against slavery. Indeed, as we read the record now, we are struck, not only with the number of church delegations who met with the President, but also with the unanimity of their concern. Lincoln did not always admire the quality of the remarks which he heard, and he felt that some of his visitors were oversure of themselves, but on the whole his admiration grew. "In a conflict which was founded on the quickened moral sense of the people," said Nicolay and Hay, "it was not strange that the Government received the most earnest support from the churches."[18]

17. Sandburg, *Abraham Lincoln, The War Years,* I, p. 555.
18. The material collected by Lincoln's two private secretaries was published first in the *Century* magazine, August, 1889, and later in *Abraham Lincoln: A History,* VI, pp. 314–342.

As Lincoln's respect for churches grew, religious people grew in their appreciation of him as their leader. That he had not actually joined a particular congregation was, in the outcome, a positive asset in this meeting of minds. Great appreciation was expressed for the numerous and profound calls to national prayer. Characteristic of the favorable response was that of Eliza Gurney, written on August 18, 1863, twelve days after the "Day of Prayer" which the President had proclaimed immediately following Gettysburg. "I can hardly refrain," wrote this devout woman, "from expressing my cordial approval of thy late excellent proclamation appointing a day of thanksgiving for the sparing and preserving mercies which, in the tender loving-kindness of our God and Savior, have been so bountifully showered upon us. . . . And I rejoice in the decided recognition of an all-wise and superintending Providence, which is so marked a feature of the aforesaid document, as well as the immediate influence and guidance of the Holy Spirit, which perhaps never in any previous state paper has been so fully recognized before."[19]

One of the most widely disseminated of all Lincoln stories is that of his outlining the one condition on which he would ever join a church. The essence of the story, in its many versions, is that he would join any church which would establish, as its sole qualification for membership, Christ's own summary of the law (Matthew 22:37–40, Mark 12:29–31, Luke 10:27). From his young manhood Lincoln had been chary of creeds, often referring to them as "man-made." In June, 1846, in his conversation with Mrs. Rankin at Petersburg Lincoln said, according to her son's report, that he had reservations about "the possibility and propriety of settling the religion of Jesus Christ in the models of man-made creeds and dogmas." Clearly, he was contrasting the creeds which he knew with the Bible, and he was well aware that

19. Eliza Gurney, *Memoir*, p. 315. Quaker visitors to President Lincoln were more numerous than any other group, Eliza Gurney being only one of many.

not one of them could be found in it. "I cannot, without mental reservations," said Lincoln, "assent to long and complicated creeds and catechisms."[20]

The most substantial source of the familiar story about the conditions of membership comes from an address given by Congressman Henry C. Deming before the General Assembly of Connecticut in 1865. Concerning Lincoln the Congressman said:

I am here reminded of an impressive remark he made to me on another occasion, which I shall never forget. He said, he had never united himself to any church, because he found difficulty in giving his assent, without mental reservations, to the long complicated statements of Christian doctrine which characterize their Articles of Belief and Confessions of Faith. "When any church," he continued, "will inscribe over its altar as its sole qualification for membership the Savior's condensed statement of the substance of both the law and the Gospel, Thou shalt love the Lord thy God with all thy heart, and with all thy soul, and with all thy mind, and thy neighbor as thyself,—that Church will I join with all my heart and soul."[21]

Even though Lincoln repeated the substance of these remarks several times, it is not easy to know how seriously to take him. It is always possible that he was partly joking, pulling the legs of his more orthodox associates. The remarks quoted are really out of character in that the mood is far more simplistic than Lincoln's mood usually was. The abbreviated creed he proposed is *necessary* for the survival of the Church of Christ, but whether it is *sufficient* is another matter. A scholarly critic is bound to observe that he included in this nothing about the life everlasting and nothing about Christ's own revelation of the Father. If we take Christ seriously, as Lincoln proposed, then we have to take seriously His words about Himself. Familiar as Lincoln was with

20. Rankin, *Personal Recollections of Abraham Lincoln*, p. 326.
21. Deming, *Eulogy upon Abraham Lincoln before the General Assembly of Connecticut* (1865), p. 42.

the Bible, he was cognizant of this aspect of Christ's teaching. The reasonable conclusion is that his repeated remark was intended chiefly to shock his listeners and to draw attention to the danger of unnecessary complexity. His theology was not, in the end, oversimplified. He recognized the delicate balance between immanence and transcendence, refusing to settle for either of these alone. In his perceptive essay, *The Meaning of God in the Life of Lincoln,* Willard L. Sperry recognized that Lincoln, though he did not explicitly formulate a creed, clearly *had* one. Referring to transcendence and immanence, Sperry said, "Now the whole deeper significance of Lincoln's religion rests in the fact that he preserved, as few men in history and none in our own history have preserved, a working balance between these two ideas, and that he used Power in Perspective. His God was a God who was both in the world and above the world."[22] A creed is what a person *believes,* and Lincoln believed something very specific. His was not religion in general. In his theological superiority "he laid hold with one hand upon the Power that comes from God at work in the world, while he clung with the other hand to God above the battle, who gave him moral and historical Perspective." Because they had superior opportunities to know the truth in these matters the tempered conclusion of his two secretaries deserves careful attention:

He was a man of profound and intense religious feeling. We have no purpose of attempting to formulate his creed; we question if he himself ever did so. There have been swift witnesses who, judging from expressions uttered in his callow youth, have called him an atheist, and others who, with the most laudable intentions, have remembered improbable conversations which they bring forward to prove at once his orthodoxy and their own intimacy with him. But leaving aside these apocryphal evidences, we have only to look at his authentic public and private utterances to see how deep and strong in all the latter part of his life was

22. P. 10.

the current of his religious thought and emotion. He continually invited and appreciated, at their highest value, the prayers of good people. The pressure of the tremendous problems by which he was surrounded; the awful moral significance of the conflict in which he was the chief combatant; the overwhelming sense of personal responsibility, which never left him for an hour—all contributed to produce, in a temperament naturally serious and predisposed to a spiritual view of life and conduct, a sense of reverent acceptance of the guidance of a Superior Power.[23]

Being neither a church member nor antichurch, Lincoln's behavior was often perplexing to both the orthodox and the heretical. While one group was shocked to find him so pious, the other was surprised to find him unimpressed by ecclesiastical rules and practices. An instance of the latter was his almost total inattention to the conventional Christian calendar. To this day there are people who can hardly believe it when they suddenly realize that Lincoln was shot while attending the theater on *Good Friday*, of all days. What a way, they say, to remember the Crufixion! The obvious answer is that it was *not* his way of remembering the Crucifixion of Christ. Special days in the church year meant almost nothing to this man of the prairie, who voted to keep the legislature in session on Christmas Day. As we study his official letters, we find that he dated some of them on Christmas and apparently made no recognition of a special festival celebrating the birth of Christ. On December 25, 1863, he wrote to Bayard Taylor, Secretary of Legation at St. Petersburg, about his lecture "Serfs, Serfdom, and Emancipation in Russia."

Lincoln's unconcern about the eccelesiastical calendar is more understandable when we realize that his practice was consistent with the general cultural pattern of his time. Today nearly everyone puts great emphasis upon Christmas, but in earlier America this was not the case. A hundred years ago schools were sometimes conducted at Christmas, precisely as on other days. It is

23. Nicolay and Hay, VI, pp. 339, 340.

hard for us to remember how recent in American experience is the recognition of Holy Week, and especially of Good Friday. There are many now living who, in their childhood, were not reminded of these days at all. Indeed, in some church circles genuine pride was taken in the refusal to make a distinction between days, on the ground that all days should be equally holy. Lincoln appears to have felt this way to the end, and in this he was truly a man of the people.

On more than one occasion President Lincoln was faced with the problem posed by the preaching of treasonable sentiments under the cloak of religious freedom. Feeling the delicacy of this problem, he deliberately practiced restraint. His policy was to make as little as possible of the issue. But in case there was flagrant defiance, he determined, as we have noted earlier, to maintain a single standard and to hold clergymen accountable to the law, exactly as in the case of other men. In regard to a congregation in Memphis, Tennessee, which was divided in loyalty, this combination of restraint and equality before the law was admirably illustrated. "I say again," Lincoln wrote on May 13, 1864, "if there be no military need for the building, leave it alone, neither putting any one in or out, of it, except on finding some one preaching or practicing treason, in which case lay hands upon him just as if he were doing the same thing in any other building, or in the streets or highways."[24] In short, his growing respect for the Church did not lead the President to favoritism. The freedom of religion, as he understood it, was a freedom that had to be exercised within the law.

One result of Lincoln's new respect for the churches was his eagerness to help church people perform services to which they felt drawn. This is why he made a pioneering decision to facilitate the work of ministers in military hospitals. He wrote to

24. *Collected Works,* VII, p. 339.

certain volunteers: "Having been solicited by Christian ministers, and other pious people, to appoint suitable persons to act as chaplains at the hospitals for our sick and wounded soldiers, and feeling the intrinsic propriety of having such persons so to act, and yet believing there is no law conferring the power upon me to appoint them, I think fit to say that if you will voluntarily enter upon and perform the appropriate duties of such position, I will recommend that Congress make compensation therefor at the same rate as chaplains in the army are compensated."[25] In similar vein the President agreed to help promote a plan for religious work among the armed forces adopted by a committee appointed by the Young Men's Christian Association.[26] On August 21, 1863, he approved a plan of "colored ministers of the Gospel, who express a wish to go within our military lines and minister to their brethren there. The object is a worthy one, and I shall be glad for all facilities to be afforded them which may not be inconsistent with or a hindrance to our military operations."[27]

Many of the churches with which Lincoln had had some connection were represented in his funeral arrangements. These included the services in the White House, the journey of twelve days and nights by train, and finally the concluding ceremony at Springfield. The long journey home reversed the trip from Springfield to Washington, more than four years before. Many remembered how he had said, as he left Springfield, "I now leave not knowing when, or whether ever, I may return." The scene was one for the depiction of which the gifts of Carl Sandburg were admirably suited:

From his White House in Washington—where it began—they carried his coffin and followed it nights and days for twelve days.

25. *Collected Works*, V, p. 53.
26. Ibid., p. 67.
27. *Collected Works*, VI, p. 401.

By night bonfires and torches lighted the right of way for a slow-going railroad train.

By day troops with reversed arms, muffled drums, multitudinous feet seeking the pivotal box with the silver handles.

By day bells tolling, bells sobbing the requiem, the salute guns, cannon rumbling their inarticulate thunder.

To Baltimore, Harrisburg, Philadelphia, New York, they journeyed with the draped casket to meet overly ornate catafalques.

To Albany, Utica, Syracuse, moved the funeral cortege always met by marches and throngs.

To Cleveland, Columbus, Indianapolis, Chicago, they took the mute oblong box, met by a hearse for convoy to where tens of thousands should have their last look.

Then to Springfield, Illinois, the old home town, the Sangamon near by, the New Salem hill top near by, for the final rest of cherished dust.[28]

There was no argument about Church and State on Wednesday, April 19, 1865, when six hundred people crowded into the East Room of the White House. One-tenth of all present were clergymen. For the ecumenical President there was an ecumenical funeral service of genuine dignity. Chief among the participants were Dr. C. H. Hall, rector of the Church of the Epiphany, Bishop Matthew Simpson of the Methodist Episcopal Church, Dr. Phineas D. Gurley, the President's own pastor, and Dr. E. H. Gray, a Baptist, who at that time was Chaplain of the United States Senate.

It was appropriate that Dr. Gurley should give the sermon in the East Room. He knew the mind of the fallen leader so well that much of Lincoln's own mood entered into the sermon. Of Lincoln the pastor said, "He remembered that 'God is in history,' and he felt that nowhere had His hand and His mercy been so marvelously conspicuous as in the history of this nation. He

28. *Abraham Lincoln, The War Years*, IV, p. 388.

hoped and he prayed that the same hand would continue to guide us, and that same mercy continue to abound to us in the times of our greatest need." Fortunately, Dr. Gurley could speak with firsthand experience, because he had been with the President many times. In the light of such intimate knowledge he added, "I speak what I know, and testify what I have often heard him say, when I affirm that that guidance and mercy were the props on which he humbly and habitually leaned; they were the best hope he had for himself and for his country."

That the final funeral sermon at Springfield should be delivered by Bishop Matthew Simpson was a natural result of Lincoln's personal admiration for the Methodist leader. When Simpson preached in the summer of 1864 in the Methodist Church at the corner of 4½ Street and F Street, the President had been able to attend. It was fortunate for the later preparation of the Second Inaugural that the topic of the sermon was "The Providence of God as Seen in Our War." In the summer of 1864, though Grant was advancing, peace still seemed endlessly elusive. After the sermon, the Bishop and the President conferred in a friendly fashion.

Matthew Simpson (1811–1884) was exactly the kind of leader whom Lincoln could admire. Before coming into Lincoln's life, Simpson had already performed a wide variety of public service. He was president of Indiana Asbury (now De Pauw University) from 1839 to 1848, and was elected Bishop in 1852. Lincoln admired not only Simpson's eloquence and his patriotism, but also his reliability as an observer. Consequently, he listened carefully to what the Bishop reported about the mood of the country. When Simpson early reported to the President, and to some of his Cabinet members, that seventy-five thousand men were but a beginning of the number needed, he was one of the first to predict that the struggle would be long and severe. Secretary Seward minimized the credibility of Simpson's remarks, asking what opportunity a clergyman could have to judge of such affairs. Edward Bates, the Attorney General, took the opposite view, maintaining that few men knew so much of the temper of the people as Bishop Simpson did. After the Cabinet meeting, Simpson and Lincoln remained together for a long time. The Bishop gave in detail his opinion of the mood, as he knew it, throughout the country.

One result of President Lincoln's high regard for Matthew Simpson was that the Bishop was asked to preach, on the day after Lincoln's second inauguration, to a distinguished congregation which filled the Hall of Representatives. The Bishop's assignment in Washington was an excellent preparation for the still more demanding assignment only a few weeks later in Illinois. The high point at Oak Ridge Cemetery, Springfield, on May 4, 1865, was the reading aloud of Lincoln's greatest speech, followed by the sermon of Bishop Simpson. The witness of the State and the witness of the Church were not the same, but they were perfectly joined at the end.

6
The Final Paradox

I have felt His hand upon me in great trials.

ABRAHAM LINCOLN

Abraham Lincoln will be remembered for many things, but he may be remembered longest for his prophetic interpretation of American history. His patriotism was of such magnitude that it cannot easily be exaggerated, but it was never idolatrous, and it was saved from idolatry by the overwhelming sense of the sovereignty of God. As the Illinois lawyer grew into a world statesman, he grew primarily by the depth of his thinking which included more than political strategy.

In his mature thinking, which became established by the end of 1862, and which continued with no essential variation until the assassination, the conception of the divine will was paramount. By this time Lincoln envisaged God's will as the primary consideration in any human decision. While God's will concerned the lives of poor struggling individuals of every race and nation, it also concerned groups and, above all, nations. From the prophets of Israel Lincoln had learned the noble idea that there can be a servant people, with a responsibility to the entire "family of man." Patriotism, in this context, became even more compelling, but it was purged of all pride. In Lincoln's understanding, the group calling did not deny the individual calling. But it was in great moral developments, such as the elimination of slavery without the destruction of the Union, that Lincoln saw the working of the divine order most clearly.

We achieve a better understanding of the way in which Lincoln's patriotism transcended local limitations when we note that two of his most perceptive interpreters, Lord Charnwood and John Drinkwater, were Englishmen. The former was convinced at the end of his careful studies that the single most powerful idea in Lincoln's mind was the idea of Providence. This idea, which had grown for years, being mentioned repeatedly in the small addresses given on the journey to Washington prior to the First Inaugural, was given its fullest statement in the addresses of the last two years of Lincoln's life. "His theology, in the narrower sense," wrote Lord Charnwood, "may be said to have been limited to an intense belief in a vast and overruling Providence."[1] Like Charnwood, John Drinkwater also saw the direction in which Lincoln grew.

> Two years of darkness and this man but grows
> Greater in resolution, more constant in compassion.[2]

It is only when we see the slavery issue in the larger theological context that we are able to understand the sometimes baffling complexity of Lincoln's attitude. Lincoln refused all along to ally himself with the simplified politics of the Abolitionists, because, though he was trying to rid the world of human slavery, that was not his only purpose. Few interpreters of Lincoln's character

1. Charnwood, *Abraham Lincoln* (Garden City, N.Y.: Garden City Publishing Co., Inc., 1917).
2. Drinkwater, *Abraham Lincoln, a Play* (Boston: Houghton Mifflin Co., 1919), p. 52.

have understood this as well as did Lord Charnwood, when he wrote, "We may regard, and himself regarded, the liberation of the slaves, which will always be associated with his name, as a part of the larger work, the restoration of his country to its earliest and noblest tradition, which alone gave permanence or worth to its existence as a nation."[3]

John Bright is remembered for his influence upon American history, both in the way he helped to avoid armed conflict between Britain and America, and also in the way he prevented the recognition of the Confederacy by Great Britain and France. But many who are familiar with the work of Bright as a statesman are not equally familiar with him as a thinker who influenced the mind of Abraham Lincoln. The fact that most of the connection was through Charles Sumner, as an intermediary, does not lessen the importance of the impact. In Bright Lincoln found a true model, an astute statesman who, like himself, had a pervading sense of the sovereignty of God. Bright's clearest statement of this position was made at Birmingham, on December 18, 1862, at the end of Lincoln's most agonizing year. "I believe," he said, "the question is in the hand, not of my hon. Friend, nor in that of Lord Palmerston, nor in that even of President Lincoln, but it is in the hand of the Supreme Ruler, who is bringing about one of those great transactions in history which men often will not regard when they are passing before them, but which they look back upon with awe and astonishment some years after they are past."[4]

As Bright indicated, and as Lincoln knew very well, it is difficult to look forward and see where the Guiding Hand is leading. But, seen in later perspective, the working out of a plan is sometimes obvious. Now enough years have elapsed for us, who belong to another generation, to see something of the pattern which

3. *Abraham Lincoln*, p. 15.
4. *Addresses of John Bright* (Everyman), p. 75.

was developing, in spite of the inadequacy of the human instruments, when these responsible men lived and made decisions which affected the destinies of millions of people then unborn. What is truly remarkable is the way in which John Bright and Abraham Lincoln could see with so much perspective even while the events were transpiring. In the midst of history they partly discerned the meaning of that history!

To question, as some have done, whether Lincoln believed in God is a clear waste of time and effort. The answer is obvious. The only valuable inquiry is that of *how* he believed. In this regard the President grew prodigiously, and in this growth John Bright was one of his many teachers. Among other things, Bright helped by his emphasis upon moral consequences. As Bright looked at history he was convinced, as had been the major prophets of Israel, that God's hand in the course of events is seen in the working out of an objective moral law. A sin as great as the sin of enslaving other people was bound, thought Bright, to have agonizing consequences for a very long time. "Is not this war," he asked, "the penalty which inexorable justice exacts from America, North and South, for the enormous guilt of cherishing that frightful iniquity of slavery, for the last eighty years?"[5]

When we consider Bright's question carefully, we are prepared to understand why Lincoln may be truly called the theologian of American anguish. The prairie lawyer answered Bright's question in the affirmative, haltingly at first, but finally with amazing firmness. He grew convinced that our universe, far from demonstrating a merely mechanical order, is a theater for the working out of the moral law. If he were alive today he would not be surprised at the continued agony which marks the relationships of black people and white people, not only in America, but also in many other parts of the world. The mills of the moral order,

5. Ibid., p. 83.

he thought, grind slowly, but they grind relentlessly. Slavery was a sin so terrible that men and women may still be paying for it a hundred years from now.

Lincoln was not, of course, alone in his understanding of the moral pattern of history with its consequent sorrow. Few who have understood the idea of Providence have spoken primarily of comfort. Lincoln's correspondent, Eliza Gurney, spoke to him not only of the ecstasy, but also of the agony. "By terrible things in righteousness," she wrote, "the Lord seems indeed to have been answering our prayers that He would make us wholly His own." More than a hundred years earlier, John Woolman, in the midst of his 1746 visit to colonies where the slave trade was common, wrote in his Journal, "I Saw in these Southern Provinces, so many Vices and Corruptions increased by this trade and this way of life, that it appeared to me as a dark gloominess hanging over the Land, and though now many willingly run into it, yet in future the Consequence will be grievous to posterity." And then, to make sure that the reader would not suppose that the journalist was expressing a temporary emotion, Woolman added, "I express it as it hath appeared to me, not at once, nor twice, but as a matter fixed on my mind."[6] Indeed, Woolman believed that the high cost of slavery, not only for the slaves, but also for owners and for the entire nation, would with the ensuing years grow greater rather than less. In 1757 he said, "I believe that burthen will grow heavier and heavier, till times change in a way disagreeable to us."[7] The events of Lincoln's administration were verifications of the truth of Woolman's remarkable prediction more than a century earlier. With Woolman and with Mrs. Gurney, Abraham Lincoln understood the concept of "terrible things in righteousness," because, like them, he knew Psalm 65:5.

6. *The Journal of John Woolman*, edited by Amelia Mott Gummere (New York: The Macmillan Company, 1922), p. 167.
7. Ibid., p. 191.

One significant aspect of Lincoln's emphasis upon God's will was his complete lack of self-righteousness. In this he was remarkably different from many of his contemporaries, especially the extreme idealists who seemed to suppose that instant Utopia was possible. He differed from the fanatical moralists primarily in that he was always perplexed. No sooner did he believe that he was doing God's will than he began to admit that God's purpose might be different from his own. In short, he never forgot the immense contrast between the absolute goodness of God and the faltering goodness of all who are in the finite predicament. It was his recognition of the universality of human fallibility that made him conscious of the dangers involved in any governmental process, including the most democratic one. There is, he saw, no possible insurance against human error. His skepticism referred even to the judicial system, which is evident from his consideration of the Dred Scott decision. Indeed, as early as July 17, 1858, he quoted Thomas Jefferson with approbation on this very point. Jefferson's words, as Lincoln quoted them, were: "Our judges are as honest as other men, and not more so. They have, with others, the same passions for party, for power, and the privilege of their corps."[8]

How early Abraham Lincoln accepted the ruling idea of the moral significance of history we cannot know, but we do know that he read *Robinson Crusoe* as a boy in Indiana, and was familiar with the words which Defoe put in Crusoe's mouth: "I ought to leave them to the justice of God, who is the governor of Nations, and knows how, by national punishments, to make a just retribution for national offences and to bring public judgments upon those who offend in a public manner, by such ways as best please him." We have reason to be grateful to Dr. Louis A. Warren for pointing out the similarity between this passage in Lincoln's boyhood reading and the Second Inaugural, produced forty-five

8. *Collected Works*, II, p. 517.

years later.[9] The words of Lincoln which parallel the words of Defoe are, "If we shall suppose that American Slavery is one of those offences, which, in the providence of God, must needs come, but which, having continued through His appointed time, He now wills to remove, and that He gives to both North and South, this terrible war, as the woe due to those by whom the offence came, shall we discern therein any departure from those divine attributes which the believers in a Living God always ascribe to Him?"

Always, in Lincoln's matured theology, there is paradox. There is sternness, yet there is also tenderness; there is melancholy, yet there is also humor; there is moral law, yet there is also compassion. History is the scene of the working out of God's justice, which we can never escape, but it is also the scene of the revelation of the everlasting mercy. Lincoln knew that, if we stress only the mercy, we become sentimentalists, while, if we stress only the justice, we are driven to despair. The secret of rationality is the maintenance of the tension. The greatest possible mistake is the fatuous supposition that we have resolved it. Scholars have noted in the passage from the Second Inaugural quoted above that the words succeed in expressing both the pious and the skeptical notes in Lincoln's matured faith. Reinhold Niebuhr drew attention to the reason why both notes were required, if the truth was to be told. Both are needed, he explained, because "the drama of history is shot through with moral meaning; but the meaning is never exact. Sin and punishment, virtue and reward are never precisely proportioned."[10] Lincoln believed in Providence, but, in Niebuhr's terms, he understood "the error of identifying providence with the cause to which the agent is committed."[11] When dedicated people forget the ubiquity of this

9. *Lincoln's Youth, Seven to Twenty-one*, pp. 68, 69, 233. The Defoe passage is quoted from *Robinson Crusoe* (London: Henry G. Bolen, 1856), p. 133.
10. Nevins, p. 74.
11. Ibid., p. 75.

danger, they are almost sure to become self-righteous. Only the person who recognizes that he is personally involved in the evils which he seeks to eliminate has any chance of avoiding this primary moral mistake. Lincoln, conscious as he was of the radical difference between the divine will and the human will, understood that ambiguities appear in the moral stance of even the most dedicated crusaders.

The character of Lincoln's intellectual achievement is better appreciated when we recognize that the combination which he demonstrated is exceedingly rare. There are many instances in history of people who allow their skepticism to cut the nerve of moral effort, and there are numerous people, on the other hand, who are fierce crusaders at the price of fanaticism. In his political commitments the fanatic makes claims for his particular cause which cannot be validated by either a transcendent Providence or a neutral posterity.

Lincoln's achievement looms the greater in our own years, since they are marked almost as much by anguish as were his own. The more we observe the failure of the obvious alternatives, i.e., spirituality without passion, and passion without perspective, the more we realize the real brilliance of Lincoln's mature solution of the problem. "It was," said Niebuhr, "Lincoln's achievement to embrace a paradox which lies at the center of the spirituality of all western culture; namely, the affirmation of a meaningful history and the religious reservation about the partiality and bias which the human actors and agents betray in the definition of meaning."[12] Both Abraham Lincoln and Jefferson Davis were patriotic and also reverent men, but there was a crucial difference between them, because Lincoln appreciated paradox as Jefferson Davis did not.

Abraham Lincoln was a patriot who was devoted to something far more profound than what is ordinarily understood as nation-

12. Ibid., p. 77.

alism. America was important in his eyes because God, he believed, had a magnificent work for America to perform, a work significant for the whole world. This, as he said at Trenton before his first inauguration, was "something that held out a great promise to all the people of the world to all time to come."[13] In calling Americans to this vision of greatness God might even go so far, he thought, as to *compel* obedience. In this conviction Lincoln's mood was similar to that of some of the Old Testament prophets. In June, 1862, the crucial month for making up his mind whether to issue the Emancipation Proclamation, he had an important confrontation with a group brought to him by James F. Wilson, Iowa Congressman and Chairman of the House Judiciary Committee.

One member of Wilson's delegation, a strong antislavery man, said to the President, "Slavery must be stricken down wherever it exists. If we do not do right I believe God will let us go our own way to our ruin. But if we do right I believe he will lead us safely out of this wilderness, crown our arms with victory, and restore our now dissevered Union." The significance of Lincoln's response lies in the way in which he picked up the man's idea of divine guidance and went beyond it. He rose slowly to his full height, "his right arm outstretched toward the gentleman who had just ceased speaking, his face aglow like the face of a prophet," reported the Congressman. To the surprise of his admonisher the President said, "My faith is greater than yours." In common with his visitor, he, too, believed in the role of God in history, but he went on to declare a new thing, to the effect that God will not abandon us to the foolishness of our own devices. "I also believe," he continued, "that He will compel us to do right in order that He may do these things, not so much because we desire them as that they accord with His plan of dealing with this

13. *Collected Works,* IV, p. 236.

nation, in the midst of which He means to establish justice. I think He means that we shall do more than we have yet done in furtherance of His plans, and He will open the way for our doing it. I have felt His hand upon me in great trials and submitted to His guidance, and I trust that as He shall further open the way, I will be ready to walk therein, relying on His help and trusting in His goodness and wisdom."[14]

The Wilson interview is clearly one of the most revealing scenes in the entire career of Abraham Lincoln. Just the experience of reading the words now is a truly ennobling one. Here we are, at last, far removed from the cracker-barrel discussions of free will, of fatalism and of foreordination, which marked the early growth of Lincoln's philosophy in Illinois. Those discussions were abstract, but what Lincoln told the delegation in June, 1862, referred with urgency to the concrete developments of history. Thinking was not an empty game; it made a difference in the course of events. Part of the paradox was that the more agonizing the decisions became, the more Lincoln was convinced that even his personal choices were being guided by Another.

It is fortunate that we possess corroborating accounts of the way in which Lincoln's convictions were developing into a mature theology during the final chapter of his life. The report of the Register of the Treasury, L. E. Chittenden (1824–1900), supplements that of the Wilson confrontation. "His calm serenity at times when others were so anxious," reported Chittenden, "his confidence that his own judgment was directed by the Almighty, so impressed me that when I next had the opportunity, at some risk of giving offence, I ventured to ask him directly how far he believed the Almighty actually directed our national affairs. There was a considerable pause before he spoke, and when he did speak, what he said was more in the nature of a monologue than

14. James F. Wilson, *North American Review*, December, 1896, pp. 668, 669.

an answer to my inquiry. 'That the Almighty does make use of human agencies, and directly intervenes in human affairs, is,' he said, 'one of the plainest statements of the Bible. I have had so many evidences of his direction, so many instances when I have been controlled by some other power than my own will, that I cannot doubt that this power comes from above. I frequently see my way clear to a decision when I have no sufficient facts upon which to found it. But I cannot recall one instance in which I have followed my own judgment, founded upon such a decision, where the results were unsatisfactory, whereas, in almost every instance where I have yielded to the views of others, I have had occasion to regret it. I am satisfied that when the Almighty wants me to do or not to do a particular thing, he finds a way of letting me know it. I am confident that it is his design to restore the Union. He will do it in his own good time.' "[15]

The paradox that man is most free when he is most guided was something which Abraham Lincoln had to work out for himself, but he was neither the first nor the last to do so. In our own century Professor Donald Baillie of St. Andrews University has reached a conclusion identical with that reached by Lincoln in the midst of national danger. "Guided freedom," said Baillie, "is a paradox, because the ascription of all the glory to God for anything good that is in us does not imply any destruction of our freedom as human personalities, but precisely the reverse: our actions are never more truly free and personal and human, they are never more truly our own, than when they are wrought in us by God."[16]

During the last months of his life Lincoln's thinking achieved a genuine synthesis. The solution to which he felt led about emancipation did not please those whose thinking was less com-

15. Chittenden, *Recollections of President Lincoln and His Administration* (New York: Harper & Brothers, 1891), p. 448.
16. Baillie, *God Was in Christ* (New York: Charles Scribner's Sons, 1955), p. 145.

plicated. Such people freely accused the President of expediency, but in this they were wrong. At the heart of the momentous decision there was a hard core of principle from which nothing could move him. What the Abolitionists condemned as expediency was really a matter of intelligent tactics and no more, and the historical outcome has justified the tactics. Referring to the Emancipation Proclamation and the criticism of its partial nature, Reinhold Niebuhr pointed out that "both its timing and its immediate scope were the fruits of statesmanlike calculations," for Lincoln, while he was a prophet, was also more than a prophet. "Lincoln's faith," said Niebuhr, "is identical with that of the Hebraic prophets, who first conceived the idea of a meaningful history," but he was also "a responsible statesman." Lincoln's philosophy was flexible. He sought to choose among the possibles and thereby do the right thing in the light of circumstances, but "all of his actions and attitudes can be explained and justified," in Niebuhr's judgment, "by his hierarchy of values."[17] He did not move at the speed for which some of his critics, such as Horace Greeley, clamored, but he was saved from moral ambiguity by absolute firmness at one central point.

Lincoln's first public statement which explained unmistakably his pivotal moral position was the Message to Congress of December 1, 1862. This Message, produced at the end of his year of greatest strain, contains the fundamental solution which he had reached. It was a solution he never questioned thereafter, though the problems continued to multiply. In this Message, which by common consent is one of Lincoln's best, the thoughtful President was really dealing with the philosophy of history. It is no wonder, then, that he began the final paragraph by saying, "Fellow-citizens, we cannot escape history." God, Lincoln believed, is seen more clearly in events than in nature, though He may be

17. Nevins, p. 83.

seen there also. It is a majestic thing, thought Lincoln, for a person to be *responsible*. "The fiery trial through which we pass, will light us down, in honor or dishonor, to the latest generation." History is never abstract because it is concerned with what persons do. "We—even *we here*—hold the power, and bear the responsibility."

The Message to Congress[18] is significant for any person who seeks to understand Lincoln's unshakable center of conviction. Some indication of this had already been revealed in the letter to Horace Greeley, written three months earlier, when the President said, "My primary purpose is to save the Union." But the words of the Message to Congress go further. What was at stake, Lincoln had come to believe, was the conception of a really free society, such as the world had never seen. He knew human selfishness too well to think that a truly free society could be easily demonstrated anywhere, but he was convinced that the development of the American Union was peculiarly fortunate in its promise. God, he believed, was trying to bring to pass something unique on American shores and prairies. The Emancipation Proclamation, scheduled to take effect in exactly one month, was frankly a war measure designed to save the Union, and, by saving the Union, to keep open the opportunity for a life of freedom on the part of all who were involved, both black and white. Flexible as he was on other points, this was the rock from which Lincoln could not be moved. This is why, when the Confederate government made its peace overtures, Lincoln would not, in spite of his desire for the cessation of hostilities, sign his name to any agreement which referred to "two nations." If it were not one nation, the hope, he thought, was destroyed. Herein lies the enduring appeal of the familiar words with which the Message to Congress ended. His theme was the indivisibility of freedom. "In *giving* freedom to the *slave*, we *assure* freedom to

18. For the entire address see *Collected Works*, V, pp. 518–537.

the free—honorable alike in what we give, and what we preserve. We shall nobly save, or meanly lose, the last best, hope of earth." With these words Lincoln had arrived. Not yet was there peace in the divided country and peace in the nation is, in one sense, still elusive today, but Abraham Lincoln had found peace in his own mind.

Reinhold Niebuhr's sober conclusion is one no thoughtful person can consider lightly. "It is, in short," he stated, "not too much to claim that Lincoln embraced the paradox of all human spirituality, and of western dynamism in particular, more adequately than any statesman of modern history."[19] The way in which Lincoln embraced the paradox is demonstrated most thoroughly in the Second Inaugural, but, meantime, it received brief expression in the Gettysburg Address. Short as the speech was, it enabled Lincoln to express the larger meaning of the conflict. As Allan Nevins said in commemoration of the Address, Lincoln was amazingly successful in communicating "his realization that the war was a desperate test on a world stage of the question whether a democracy of continental dimensions and idealistic commitments could triumphantly survive or must ignobly collapse."[20]

Before the Gettysburg battle such a definitive statement as that of November 19, 1863, would have been premature. But, after Gettysburg, Lincoln saw that in spite of sorrows yet to come the outcome was reasonably certain. The second time that Lee's army crossed the Potomac River into Virginia was the last. Accordingly, Lincoln, as the chief architect of victory, felt the time had come to make a definitive statement. He welcomed the opportunity and prepared carefully, even though all that he said can be printed, without difficulty, on one page. The second of Lincoln's three theological documents is much the shortest.

We know something of how the Gettysburg Address was pre-

19. Nevins, p. 87.
20. Ibid., p. 5.

pared because there are five copies, each one different and each in Lincoln's own handwriting. Edward Everett's long oration was an excellent one, but it would not even be remembered apart from the fact that the orator shared the platform with the President, who was not expected to do anything except to make a formal dedication of the battlefield. Everett's magnanimity is shown by his saying in a letter to the President, "I should be glad if I could flatter myself that I came as near to the central idea of the occasion in two hours, as you did in two minutes."[21] Lincoln's letter to Everett, dated Washington, November 20, 1863, was equally magnanimous. "In our respective parts yesterday," he wrote, "you could not have been excused to make a short address nor I a long one. I am pleased to know that, in your judgment, the little I did say was not entirely a failure."[22]

Lincoln could have no way of estimating the enduring significance of his address. Part of it was written in Washington, before he took the train about noon on the 18th. The writing was completed in Gettysburg, the last touches being added between nine and ten o'clock of the 19th in the home of Judge David Wills, his Gettysburg host. Contrary to a popular legend, no part of the speech appears to have been written on the train. The brevity of the utterance was in marked contrast to the magnitude of the purpose. We can rightly be appreciative of the insight of Allan Nevins who has seen that Lincoln "chose to speak not to his country alone but to aspirants for freedom in all countries, and not to his own moment in history but to the centuries. The proposition that all men are created equal was a truth for the ages, and if America, under God, achieved a new birth of freedom, it would stand as an object lesson to all nations."[23]

Lincoln was somewhat disappointed in the reaction received,

21. *Collected Works*, VII, p. 25.
22. Ibid., p. 24
23. Nevins, p. 11.

even though he was four times interrupted by applause. The message was too powerful for his hearers to grasp its significance immediately, but there was, nevertheless, long-continued hand-clapping at its conclusion. How could the people standing there on the battlefield know that they were listening to some of the greatest words of the world? Because their expectation was that he would merely pronounce a formal dedication, it took some time for his fellow citizens to realize that the wartime President had done so much more. What had he done? The answer of Allan Nevins, in his Introduction to the commemorative volume produced after a century, is very impressive. Lincoln, he says, "had dedicated the nation to the defense and invigoration of free institutions wherever the influence of the republic might extend." It is not really surprising that, at first, only a few appreciated that Lincoln "had written one of the noblest prose poems of the language."

Of all the effective phrases in the well-known address, none is more revealing of the inner life of Lincoln than the words "under God." Since these words did not appear in the original version, we are driven to the conclusion that they were added extempore, as Lincoln rose to the occasion. The newspaper version includes the words "under God," as do the versions copied later, including the one which the President sent to Edward Everett on February 4, 1864.

When Lincoln inserted the now familiar phrase it was not in general use. In our time we have honored Lincoln's new phrase by making it an official part of the Salute to the Flag, but on November 19, 1863, it appeared to be merely a fortunate interpolation. Consideration of these words is necessary for any who try to probe the depths of Lincoln's understanding of the role of God's will in history. We cannot know all that Lincoln meant, but we can at least know that he was seeking to express a nonidolatrous patriotism and that he achieved this by the conviction that the nation, good as it may be, is never really supreme. All that we do as men and as patriots is seen in perspective when we realize that all of us are "under judgment."

The inspired interpolation in the Gettysburg Address was not, of course, Lincoln's first employment of the idea. Far from inserting something strange, he was expressing in the briefest manner possible the quintessence of his thinking on the major issue. The idea of the "almost chosen people" had finally come to flower after two and a half years of intellectual struggle. Lincoln was able to employ the words without prior intent, because they were already deeply embedded in his consciousness. On May 13, 1862, when he addressed the soldiers of the Twelfth Indiana Regiment, thanking the men for their sacrificial support of "free government and free institutions," he added "For the part that you and the brave army of which you are a part have, under Providence, performed in this great struggle, I tender more thanks."[24] The term "under Providence" is not identical with the term used at Gettysburg, but the meaning is similar.

Much earlier, indeed in his boyhood, the specific words "under God" evidently came to Lincoln's attention. The version of the Bible which young Lincoln read so avidly was, of course, that dedicated to King James in 1611. In the dedication, normally printed in all editions, the phrase appears in the following context: The translators address the King, not as absolute sovereign, but as the one "who, under God, is the immediate Author of their true happiness."

Today Lincoln's address is far better known than are the events which it was written to commemorate. Thousands now read the words on the interior wall of the Lincoln Memorial in Washington. Even in London, at the Church of St. Clement Danes, in the Strand, American tourists are surprised to find part

24. *Collected Works*, V, p. 213.

of it inscribed as an inspiration to all who will take the trouble
to read. "The speech," said Charles Sumner, "will live when the
memory of the battle will be lost or only remembered because of
the speech."

President Lincoln's address on the occasion of his second
inauguration has often been called the greatest state paper of the
nineteenth century, but it is more than a state paper; it has
already become a theological classic. Its length is in marked contrast to that of the First Inaugural, which was five times as long.
The President began by explaining this contrast. Four years
earlier it had seemed fitting and proper, he said, to state somewhat in detail the nature of the course which he expected to
pursue, but in 1865 that need no longer existed. It did not exist
because, during the intervening months, public declaration had
"been constantly called forth on every point and phase of the
great contest." Consequently, there was little new to be presented. The sad truth which Lincoln had had to face as he began
his first term was recollected in an unforgettable manner. "Both
parties deprecated war; but one of them would *make* war rather
than let the nation survive; and the other would *accept* war rather
than let it perish. And the war came." In this last sentence of only
four syllables is the quintessence of Lincoln's literary style.

The longest paragraph of the Second Inaugural is devoted to
a theological analysis of the conflict which was so much more
than a series of battles. No one knew better than did Lincoln how
doubtful the outcome had been. Paul H. Douglas, former Senator
from Illinois, has shown, sensitively, what consequences de-
pended upon the outcome at Gettysburg in July, 1863. If there
were draft riots in New York ten days *after* the Union victory
at Gettysburg, "what would they have done," asks Douglas, "had
Gettysburg been a Northern defeat?" The Copperhead movement was strong, with powerful organs in the New York *World*

and the Chicago *Times.* Lord Palmerston would have welcomed an excuse to recognize the Confederacy.

"The turning of the Union flanks and the defeat of the Union army at Gettysburg, therefore," says Senator Douglas, "might well have meant the loss of the war with all the incalculable consequences which would have meant the creation of two hostile nations in the middle of North America, one dedicated to slavery and the other to freedom. The former would have inevitably sought to create a slave empire so that as southern soil became exhausted, the slaves could then be taken to Mexico, to Central America, and to the sugar-rich islands of the Caribbean. North America would then have become another Europe with deadly wars periodically waged between the two contending nations. Athens and Sparta would have again been locked in internecine warfare, and Gettysburg would have been but a prelude to still greater struggles on a continent drenched with blood."[25]

The wonder of history is that what Senator Douglas has described so vividly did not occur, for *the Union was preserved.* How, the pensive Lincoln asked, was this possible? Certainly it did not come about as a consequence of the supreme wisdom or righteousness of the citizens of the North. The only reasonable explanation, in Lincoln's mature thought, was that of the Guiding Hand of God. The occasion on March 4, 1865, gave Lincoln his best opportunity to state the Biblical faith which, by this time, had come to form the center of his conviction. He included fourteen references to God, many scriptural allusions, and four direct quotations from the Bible.[26] It is difficult to think of another state paper so steeped in Scripture and so devoted to theological reflection.

Readers in both America and abroad were quick to recognize

25. Nevins, p. 99.
26. The passages quoted are Genesis 3:19, Matthew 7:1, Matthew 18:7, and Psalm 19:9.

the greatness of Lincoln's last major utterance. The praise expressed by the London *Spectator* was unqualified. "We cannot read it," said the *Spectator* after Lincoln's death, "without a renewed conviction that it is the noblest political document known to history, and should have for the nation and the statesman he left behind him something of a sacred and almost prophetic character. Surely, none was ever written under a stronger sense of the reality of God's government, and certainly none written in a period of passionate conflict ever so completely excluded the partiality of victorious faction, and breathed so pure a strain of mingled justice and mercy." Such a generous judgment makes us realize that the opinion makers of England had moved a long way since the time when John Bright had stood virtually alone in his support of Abraham Lincoln. Even the London *Times*, after a four-year record of pro-Confederate bias, reported the speech favorably.

The key sentence of the entire utterance appears in the middle of the long paragraph, "The Almighty has His own purposes." This is what Lincoln was already sensing in September, 1862, after the second catastrophe at Bull Run, when many believed that defeat was inevitable and the sad-eyed son of the prairie wrote the "Meditation on the Divine Will"; but not until the end was virtually in sight was he able to say it so simply. Here, near the close of the drama, he was verifying what he had said twenty-eight months earlier in the presence of Mrs. Gurney and others, "though with our limited understandings we may not be able to comprehend it, yet we cannot but believe that he who made the world still governs it."

If there has ever been any doubt about Lincoln's conception of God being personal, the Second Inaugural dispels that doubt. He refers without ambiguity to the "Living God." This is far removed from any philosophical system which sees God as an impersonal Force. God, as envisaged in the Second Inaugural, is personal because He has a "will," and "living" because He makes a difference in contemporary history. The personal understanding of God's will separates Lincoln's thinking from the fatalism which he sometimes discussed in his youthful speculations.

Previews of the Second Inaugural Address came at many points in Lincoln's development. One of the most admired phrases is "with malice toward none," but he had already employed this idea earlier. At the close of a letter written July 28, 1862, the rejection of malice was specifically mentioned. In the letter he said: "I am in no boastful mood. I shall not do *more* than I can, and I shall do *all* I can to save the government, which is my sworn duty as well as my personal inclination. I shall do nothing in malice. What I deal with is too vast for malicious dealing."[27]

What Lincoln did superbly on March 4, 1865, was to give definitive form to ideas with which he was already familiar. One preview appeared eleven months earlier, on April 4, 1864, in a letter to Albert G. Hodges, editor of the Frankfort, Kentucky, *Commonwealth*. As in so many other productions, including the Second Inaugural itself, the essence is in the final paragraph. "If God now wills the removal of a great wrong," he concluded, "and wills also that we of the North as well as you of the South, shall pay fairly for our complicity in that wrong, impartial history will find therein new cause to attest and revere the justice and goodness of God."[28] Only a slight development was required to give us the sentence which we know so well and which has already been quoted in this chapter.

Glad as readers are to know the reaction of people in America and in other countries to Lincoln's address, no criticism is more interesting than Lincoln's own estimate of his most ambitious literary effort. Fortunately, we know what he thought, because

27. *Collected Works*, V, p. 346.
28. *Collected Works*, VII, p. 282.

he expressed himself eleven days after the Inauguration to the journalist Thurlow Weed. The letter not only shows that, in spite of humility, he could make a just estimate of his own work, but also provides further insight into the thinking which lay behind the speech.

My dear Sir.

Every one likes a compliment. Thank you for yours on my little notification speech, and on the recent Inaugeral Address. I expect the latter to wear as well as —perhaps better than —anything I have produced; but I believe it is not immediately popular. Men are not flattered by being shown that there has been a difference of purpose between the Almighty and them. To deny it, however, in this case, is to deny that there is a God governing the world. It is a truth which I thought needed to be told; and as whatever of humiliation there is in it falls most directly on myself, I thought others might afford for me to tell it.

Yours truly,

A. Lincoln.[29]

The assassination of Lincoln was tragic when it came, but it would have been far more tragic if it had occurred two months earlier. Then America would have been deprived, not only of Lincoln's personal leadership, but also of a compendium of his thought. Lord Charnwood, as he meditated upon the sequence of events, recognized the existence of a dramatic pattern. "Here, " he said, "is one of the few speeches ever delivered by a great man at the crisis of his fate on the sort of occasion which a tragedian telling his story would have devised for him."[30]

One of the most revealing features of Lincoln's Second Inaugural is its intimation of what his policy would have been after the war, if he had survived. He would have treated Southerners as though they had never left the Union. One who saw this clearly was Sir Winston Churchill, who pointed out that "the death of

29. *Collected Works*, VIII, p. 356.
30. Charnwood, *Abraham Lincoln*, p. 438.

Lincoln deprived the Union of the guiding hand which alone could have solved the problems of reconstruction and added to the triumph of armies those lasting victories which are gained over the hearts of men."[31] At the Cabinet meeting on April 14, 1865, the very day on which he was shot, the President spoke of Robert E. Lee and other Confederate leaders with kindness. The assassin's bullet hurt the entire nation, but it hurt the southern part of the nation most of all. In Lincoln's last public address, given on April 11, 1865, three days before the assassination, he spoke directly of reconstruction after the war, saying that the problems it presented had pressed closely upon his attention. Then, in one of his laconic sentences, he added, "It is fraught with great difficulty."[32]

Nothing in Lincoln's theology made him expect Utopia. He did not claim that the victory of the Union forces would necessarily produce the full liberation of people, black and white. All that he claimed was that such a victory would provide *opportunity*, while defeat would entail unmitigated disaster. He accepted the basic philosophy of the Founding Fathers, including the idea of a special destiny for America, but he was sufficiently acquainted with human failure to know that progress is never certain, as it is never easy. His only certainty lay in the conviction that God will never cease to call America to her true service, not only for her own sake but for the sake of the world. He desired unity and he knew that vision is the secret of unity. Consequently, his final appeal was for the completion of what he interpreted as a holy calling. This is the significance of the admonition, "Let us strive on to finish the work we are in." Knowing that the American experiment was incomplete, he was keenly aware of the appeal produced by any structure which is only partly finished and

31. Winston Churchill, *The American Civil War* (New York: Dodd, Mead and Co., 1961), pp. 132, 133.
32. *Collected Works*, VIII, p. 400.

which, accordingly, cries out for completion. He did not predict an end to American anguish, but he did see the possibility of a determination "to do all which may achieve and cherish a just, and a lasting peace, among ourselves, and with all nations."

Index

74 75 10 9 8 7 6 5 4